Virginia Connally, M.D.

Trailblazing Physician,
Woman of Faith

Loretta Fulton

LORETTA FULTON

FOREWORD BY MARV KNOX

ISBN 978-0-578-08569-2 (pblk.: alk.paper)

© 2011, Loretta Fulton
lorettafulton@suddenlink.net
All rights reserved

Printed in the U.S.A.

Edited by Larry Zelisko

Book designed by Monte Hist
Hist & Fritz Creative Media, Inc.

Cover photos
Abilene Reporter-News

Connally Family

Other photos provided by

Abilene Reporter-News

Hardin-Simmons University

Tommy Metthe

First Baptist Church

LSU Medical Alumni Association:
A History of LSU School of Medicine–New Orleans, by
Russell C. Klein, MD, and Victoria Barreto Harkin, MA
(Authorhouse, 2010)

Connally Family

CONTENTS

Acknowledgments

A list of acknowledgments must begin and end with Virginia Connally. If not for her saying "yes" to this project, it would not have happened. My gratitude to her is beyond measure. She graciously sat for hours as I interviewed her and she dug through boxes and stacks of files in search of records and photos to assist me. If she ever grew weary of my persistence, she never let on.

As with any worthwhile endeavor, numerous people played a role. Virginia and I could not have produced this book without the assistance of countless people. A list of names always is dangerous. No doubt someone will be overlooked and for that I apologize.

But some people who must be recognized include:

- Family members who contributed memories, comments, and photos.
- Larry Zelisko, a longtime co-worker at the *Abilene Reporter-News* and an outstanding editor who made sure every comma was accounted for and every odd spelling double-checked.
- Cheerful employees of the Abilene Public Library who pointed me to the right files and guided me through the intricacies of threading a microfilm reader.
- Betsy Tyson, Archivist and Exhibits Coordinator for the Texas Medical Association in Austin, who assisted me with research in the TMA archives.
- Marv Knox, a Hardin-Simmons University graduate, editor of the Baptist Standard, and a longtime friend of Virginia who wrote the foreword.
- Staff of the alumni office at Hardin-Simmons University who located yearbooks from Virginia's years on campus and assisted with other research.
- Pat Evans, executive vice president, Taylor-Jones-Haskell-Callahan County Medical Society, who assisted with researching records.

FOREWORD

The location of Virginia Connally's bedroom speaks volumes about her character. At the dawn of 2007, she slept on the ground floor of her Abilene home, where she had maintained a bedroom for decades. But that was the year she learned about plans for the New Baptist Covenant, a coalition of Baptist conventions from across North America, pulled together by former U.S. President Jimmy Carter. The New Baptist Covenant embraced the four major African-American Baptist conventions, as well as a range of predominantly white groups. They announced a convocation to be held in Atlanta, Georgia, in early 2008, where they intended to span the racial chasm that had divided Baptists since before the Civil War.

So, Virginia did what any self-respecting 94-year-old West Texan who still lived alone would do. She moved her bedroom upstairs.

"I decided I just had to attend the New Baptist Covenant convocation.What kind of Baptist would not want to be there to participate in reconciliation between the races?" she said, explaining her intra-home relocation. Her eyes twinkled ever brighter as she continued: "Well, you know the convention center there in Atlanta is absolutely huge. It's monstrous. And the last thing I wanted was for someone to push me around in a wheelchair because I wasn't strong enough to walk. As I thought about that, I decided to move my bedroom up to the second floor. I figured climbing the stairs several times a day would build up my legs, and then getting around in Atlanta would be no problem."

And it wasn't. Virginia had a ball with the Baptists –"red, brown, yellow, black and white," as children used to sing–who assembled to celebrate unity in Christ amidst diversity in race and ethnicity.

Her move represents Virginia Connally in one climb up a flight of stairs. Imagine a different quality, value or personality trait for each step: Independent. Purposeful. Optimistic. Committed Christian. Reconciling. Tenacious. Brilliant. Creative. Loving and lovable. Humorous. Insightful. Disciplined. Curious. Considerate of others. Brave. Thoughtful. Loyal Baptist. Strong. Logical. Adventuresome.

Dedicated. Absolutely unique. Gracious. Faithful. As you trace her steps–up those stairs that strengthened her legs or throughout the journey of her long and productive life–you recognize this is a remarkable woman.

That's why I've thoroughly enjoyed reading this biography. Virginia is an inspiration. Everyone who has had the privilege of calling her a friend would add she is a blessing, too.

Loretta Fulton, a longtime reporter for the *Abilene Reporter-News* and a longtime friend of Virginia's, tells the tale of a pioneer, a community leader, a healer, a mother, a friend, a philanthropist, a church stalwart, a woman of grace and endurance.

An encyclopedia entry about Virginia Connally certainly would begin by stating the most obvious fact of her life: "first female physician in Taylor County, Texas, U.S.A." She exhibited exceptional grit and determination, to say nothing of intelligence and steadfastness, to earn a medical degree and to hang out her shingle long before the Women's Liberation Movement mainstreamed females into virtually all vocations and professions. We may take Virginia's virtues for granted today, but when she trained for and launched her professional career, many folks took them for impudence. According to the conventional wisdom of that day, women in medical school and medical practice didn't "know their place" in culture and society. Today, we can look back and thank God that Virginia and women like her didn't allow others to define their "place." We also can be grateful she and her colleagues went on to become gifted doctors. They not only moved the gender boundaries, but they also raised the bars for qualifying excellence. Too bad every young girl doesn't have the opportunity to meet Virginia, because her life is a testimony to the fact a woman can become anything she sets her mind to be.

Actually, that's a lesson for women and men alike. And anyone who's ever received a pep talk from Virginia knows it's true. Volumes could be written about lessons to be learned from her life. (And, hey, you're holding one in your hands!) But if you'll permit me, I'd like to mention four:

• THE IMPORTANCE OF INVESTING YOUR LIFE IN OTHERS Wherever Virginia has gone, she's placed the stamp of her life upon people and important causes. Think about the medical community, of course, but also the Abilene Woman's Club, First Baptist Church of Abilene, the city's universities and countless individuals. For decades and decades, she has been generous with her time, her money, her influence and her concern. The true testimony of Virginia's well-lived life is not a singular, albeit significant, accomplishment she achieved in 1940, when she opened her medical practice. It's more than that; it's the people who make others' lives better because Virginia improved and strengthened theirs.

• THE SIGNIFICANCE OF FRIENDSHIP We could write a book about Virginia's acts of kindness. Actually, I could fill a chapter by myself. But I'll tell one quick story. The temperature in Abilene spiked above 100 on the day my older daughter, Lindsay, moved into the freshmen girls' dorm at Hardin-Simmons University on the north side of Abilene. Brand-new coeds and their parents huffed and puffed and sweated buckets as we moved all those girls into their rooms. In the midst of the chaos, a student worker came up to me and said, "Mr. Knox, a Dr. Connally is downstairs to see you." Actually, it was "the" Dr. Connally. Just three months shy of her 90th birthday, Virginia put on a suit, went out and bought a beautiful bouquet of flowers, and hand-delivered them to Lindsay's dorm. She did it because we were friends. And because she wanted my daughter–whom she had not yet met–to know she had a friend in Abilene, and she never had to feel alone.

• THE VALUE OF LIFELONG LEARNING Several hundred people filled a banquet hall the day the Abilene Woman's Club presented its inaugural Legacy Award to Dr. Virginia Boyd Connally. One of the speakers described how Virginia always is learning something new and how avidly she devours books. Then the speaker started talking about how Virginia always buys multiple copies of books she's reading, because she wants others to discover what she's learning. And then the speaker asked the question we knew was coming: "How many of you have received at least one book from Virginia? Raise your hand if she's given you one or more books." Almost every person in the room raised a hand. Virginia always has been generous with her knowledge. In fact, I strive to be up on current events, theology and Baptist goings–on when I visit her, because I know she'll be on top of all those subjects, and others, and she'll want to dissect them all. Talking to Virginia always is intellectually and emotionally invigorating.

• THE ART OF AGING GRACEFULLY Virginia started blazing trails when she was very young, and she's never stopped. Her legacy in medicine is secure. Her reputation in Abilene and among Baptists is sterling. Her family and friends will remember her with fondness and love all their days. But perhaps her greatest contribution has been showing hundreds, probably thousands, of friends and acquaintances how to walk through the late years of life. She built her legs up so she could walk all over the convention center in Atlanta. But more importantly, she has maintained her intellectual stamina, native curiosity, generous humor, galactic optimism and daily can–do spirit for almost a century.

As we examine her life, may we heed her example.

Marv Knox
Dallas, Texas

INTRODUCTION

"Not any one person will ever know the whole story of Virginia Connally."
—Peggy Powell, Dallas, Texas

Peggy Powell's observation couldn't be truer. When I approached Virginia in the summer of 2008 about writing her biography, I did so with eyes wide open. At the time Virginia was 95. By the time this book was printed, she had reached 98.

No one could live that long without stories to tell of things they had done, places they had visited, and people they had known. And then there's Virginia. Her life experiences would be hard to trump—from earning a medical degree in the 1930s and opening a solo practice in 1940 to hobnobbing with heads of state to traveling the world over—Virginia has done it all.

But our first formal interview in August 2008 didn't start with any of those points. It started with a question that is the true hallmark of Virginia, one that tells where her heart lies. That question was far removed from her impressive lists of "firsts," including being Abilene's first woman doctor, her brushes with power and fame, or her far-flung travels. "Where is God in this?" was the first question Virginia asked me—before I had the opportunity to ask her my first question.

We discussed the question, and she was satisfied that the book I planned to write would reflect her love of God throughout and would leave no doubt that she knows in her heart that God is at the center of all that she has accomplished. Anyone who has met Virginia knows instinctively the answer to the question, "Where is God in this?" God is everywhere in "this" and all endeavors that Virginia undertakes.

Peggy and Boone Powell are longtime friends of Virginia dating back to when Boone Powell was administrator of Hendrick Medical Center and the couple knew Virginia at First Baptist Church. While Peggy Powell's comment, "Not any one person will ever know the whole story of Virginia Connally," certainly is true, I count it as a high honor that Virginia entrusted at least a glimpse of her life to my hands.

As we got months and months deeper into the researching of the book, I heard Virginia occasionally make a remark when someone would ask her a question about her remarkable life. "Ask Loretta Fulton," she would say. "She knows more about me than I do." It is a comment I hold dear.

Book after book could be written and still "the whole story of Virginia Connally" would not be told. The following chapters hopefully will portray at least a part of Virginia's story–the story of a trailblazing physician and a woman of deep faith who has led a distinguished life, always with God at the center.

About the Author

 Loretta Fulton earned a bachelor of journalism degree from the University of Texas at Austin in May 1969. She started work at the *Abilene Reporter-News* in September of that year and spent most of her career there, retiring in June 2007. She now is a freelance writer in Abilene, Texas. From 1997 to 2004, Fulton was the religion and higher education writer for the *Reporter-News* and it was during that time that she got to know–and appreciate–Virginia Connally.

Virginia, left, and her sister, "Babe" Ruth.

Virginia holds her brother Lee Jr. for a portrait.

BY LORETTA FULTON

Chapter 1
THE FIRST OF MANY FIRSTS

"She's the poster child for a lifelong learner."
∽ Bill Arnold, president, Texas Baptist Missions Foundation

The small headline didn't make much of a splash, hidden on Page 7 of the Social Activities section of the September 22, 1940, issue of the *Abilene Reporter-News*. "Woman Doctor Opens Office" was all it said. The brief story that followed announced the arrival of "Abilene's only woman medical doctor." Dr. Virginia H. Boyd, the article's lead paragraph stated succinctly, "yesterday announced opening of offices in the Mims building. Her practice will be limited to diseases of the eye, ear, nose and throat." Thus, Abilene, Texas' first- and only at the time–female doctor made her entry into the city's colorful history. As the years passed, Virginia would come to receive her proper acclaim. But little notice was paid in September 1940. The announcement of Virginia's historic arrival could hardly compete with larger notices on the same page of the newspaper featuring stories of Gary Cooper, one of America's favorite cowboys, starring in "The Westerner" at the Paramount Theater and Johnny Weissmuller, America's favorite Lord of the Jungle, starring in "Tarzan Finds A Son!" at the Texas.[1] But by the time Dr. Virginia Hawkins Boyd, who would become Dr. Virginia Boyd Connally following a divorce and re-marriage, retired in 1982, the newspaper's morgue files would contain stacks of clippings–much larger than the original–about her achievements.

And her press clippings wouldn't be limited to the local newspaper. Her involvement with the Baptist church, from her home church in Abilene to the world mission stage, would garner her mention in that denomination's publications. Her name would spread even further with her later service on the University of Texas School of Nursing Advisory Council and the National Board of the Medical College of Pennsylvania, established in 1850 as the Female Medical College of Pennsylvania, the first in the world for women physicians.[2] Her marriage to Abilene oilman Ed Connally, who served as chairman of the Texas Democratic Party when Lyndon Johnson was in power, would put the couple's travels and political involvement in state and national publications. By the time she took down her shingle, Dr. Virginia Boyd Connally would add a number of "firsts" to her name in addition to being Abilene's first female physician. She would become the first female chief of staff at Hendrick Medical Center, first chairman of the staff at the now-closed St. Ann Hospital, first female president of what is now the Taylor-Jones-Haskell-Callahan County Medical Society, and among the first group of women deacons at First Baptist Church. She also was the inaugural recipient of a number of local awards, including: 1988 Pathfinders Award given by the YWCA and the *Abilene Reporter-News*, Abilene Woman's Club's Legacy Award in 2009, Virtue Award given by the Round Table organization at Hardin-Simmons University in 2011, and the first woman to receive the Pioneer in Medicine award given in 2004 by the local medical society.

But before there were any "firsts" for Dr. Virginia Boyd Connally, there was Ada Virginia Hawkins, daughter of Lee and Stella Hawkins, and sister to Bartow, who died of pneumonia at age 3; Lee Jr.; Ruth, nicknamed "Babe Ruth"; and Francis, a sister whose name was spelled in the masculine to honor a relative. Virginia, still called "Sissy" by family members, was born December, 4, 1912, in the family home at 614 North Eighth Street in Temple, Texas. Plenty of things were happening that day in Temple–and the rest of the world–as recorded in the December 5, 1912, edition of *The Temple Daily Telegram*.[3] National stories like one about a sugar refining trust inquiry in Louisiana shared front page space with local stories about the launching of the Empty Stocking Crusade on behalf of needy children at Christmastime. Also on the same day that the future "first female physician in Abilene" was born, the Temple newspaper reported that the local medical society met, elected officers, and heard a paper read on "Eye Injury." Who could have predicted that 25 years later, a baby born that day at 614 North Eighth Street in Temple, Texas, would graduate from Louisiana State University School of Medicine, embark on a career in treating diseases of the eye, ear, nose and throat, and become the first female physician in Abilene? Virginia certainly would not have predicted it for herself. Nothing in her early years pointed in that direction. The only class she took in high school remotely related to a career in medicine was Latin. But she didn't have medicine in mind when she signed up. She only took the class because she liked the teacher.

The Hawkins family lived in the house where Virginia was born until she reached high school, then made a short move to a larger, two-story home at 604 North Eighth Street. Even though the house was larger, it still had only one bathroom. "You took turns," Virginia recalled with a laugh. Virginia remembered sharing a bedroom, as well as hopes and dreams, with her sisters. The family faithfully attended First Baptist Church, where Stella Hawkins taught Sunday School. Wednesday night prayer meetings were routine and Virginia "never thought of not going." Religion was such a part of the family life that Virginia and her sister Ruth knew what their future would hold if for some reason they were left without family. "We thought that if we were ever left alone, we would be missionaries," she remembered. Virginia never became a full-time missionary, but she did take part in medical mission trips to Venezuela, served on a regional development council for the Foreign Mission Board of the Southern Baptist Convention, was a member of the inaugural board of the Texas Baptist Missions Foundation, and, when she established her medical practice, financially supported a young female patient who wanted to become a missionary. She routinely visited missionaries in various parts of the world as she traveled for business or pleasure. At one time, Virginia even owned the house next door to hers so that it could be used to house missionaries on furlough in Abilene. To most people, that would seem an incredibly generous act, but not to Virginia. Typically, she downplayed her charity, reasoning that, "You can't outgive God."

But long before any of that, Virginia was a girl growing up in Temple, a Central Texas city about 70 miles north of the state's capital city, Austin. She spent much of her time reading. The daily newspaper and *McCall's* magazine were household staples. She loved English but wasn't interested in science. She did well in school, routinely making the honor roll. She loved school, but college wasn't even a thought in those early school years. "You just did what was right in front of you," she said. As a child, she was close to her mother, but also enjoyed making delivery trips with her father, an independent oil and gasoline distributor. Stops were made in nearby communities, sometimes at "filling stations" and other times at small grocery stores with one pump out front. She remembered one trip when she was about six years old. The delivery truck was running low on gas, so her father just pulled over and took care of it. "I was amazed when he would go back to the back and get a can and come back and fill up," Virginia recalled, the amazement still evident at the thought of that long ago "magic."

Virginia's young years were spent in a loving home that was typical of small-town American life in those days. Mary Anne Barker of Dallas, formerly of Abilene, recalled that her parents moved to Temple a few months before she was born and lived next door to the Hawkins family. She remembered her parents speaking admiringly of the family next door. "Mother just thought so much of them," Barker said. Her mother, Lorena Nash Campbell, described Stella Hawkins as "a fast-moving woman who was on top of everything from early in the morning." In Virginia's younger days, her mother constantly was hanging out the wash or tending to the myriad chores required to keep a large household running smoothly, Barker's mother told her. Later during World War II, upstairs bedrooms in the house once occupied by Hawkins children were rented to wives of soldiers stationed at nearby Fort Hood.

Even if Virginia didn't think much about college during

Standing in back is Virginia's brother, Lee Jr. Seated left to right are sister "Babe" Ruth, Virginia, sister Francis, and their mother, Stella Hawkins.

her younger years growing up in Temple, a decision had to be made when she graduated high school in 1929 at age 16, the young age due to an early start date. Temple Junior College was the logical choice, and Virginia enrolled for one year. Virginia's mother had a brother, Dr. William Riley Snow and his wife, Mae Cagle Snow, who lived in Abilene. The couple had located there following Dr. Snow's military service. They chose the West Central Texas city where Mae's parents lived and her father was a Baptist minister. The city also was home to three institutions of higher learning, including a Baptist institution, Simmons University, now Hardin-Simmons University. Will and Mae wanted Virginia to live with them and attend Simmons University. "He wanted all his nieces and nephews to get a degree," Virginia recalled. So off to Abilene

Virginia went. She and a cousin from Fort Worth, who also was a Simmons student, shared the Snow home at 1210 North Eighteenth Street. Virginia recalled the home being a large two-story white house with gorgeous trees around it. It later was demolished to make room for the Dawson Medical Building, which still stood in 2011. The building was constructed in 1987 and occupied for many years by Dr. George Dawson, whose general practice overlapped Virginia's practice from 1959 until her retirement in 1982.

It didn't take long to settle into the life of a college student. Virginia had all the encouragement she needed from her parents and her aunt and uncle, who recognized her potential. She recalled a favorite "warning" from her aunt. "Virginia," Mae would say, "don't let me ever catch you without something to read." That bit of advice stuck with Virginia, and years later she would pass on her passion for reading to her only child, Ann Virginia (Genna) Boyd Davis, who was born May 9, 1944, in Temple. Among Genna's fondest childhood memories are of her mother reading her to sleep. Virginia would read anything to her daughter, from medical journals to the Bible. "Sometimes, we would discuss what she thought," Genna recalled, "and she would ask me for my opinion." Virginia's reading habits haven't changed much over the years. Even now, in her late 90s, she constantly reads and shares books and articles with friends. "She's a voracious reader," a friend, Bill Arnold, president of the Texas Baptist Missions Foundation, observed. Virginia was a charter member of the foundation's board of advisors in 1992 and now is a member emeritus. Virginia met Arnold in 1984, when the Foundation was established, and he soon took note of her intellect and her constant reading habits. "But more than just being a reader, she's a thinker," he said. "She's the poster child for a lifelong learner."

Favorite readings include the Bible, daily newspapers, correspondence, and books on politics, spirituality, or any new topic that might catch her attention. An almost daily staple since 1975 has been *My Utmost for His Highest*, a book of daily meditations and Scriptures written by Oswald Chambers and originally published in 1935. The book was given to Virginia on February 11, 1975, by a patient, Irene Fanson. Virginia's well-worn copy is filled with small Post-it® notes that record new personal insights she gets daily from reading the meditations, even after all these years. She recalled sitting in a hospital room in Houston on August 10, 1975, with her husband, Ed, who would die 11 days later. "Self-pity is of the devil," was the essence of the Scripture and meditation for the day. Virginia took it to heart, moving forward as president of Connally Oil Company in addition to maintaining her daily medical practice after Ed died. Virginia's love of books is legendary, and showed up in numerous comments recorded in publications over the years. In 1992, the *Abilene Reporter-News*, Virginia's hometown newspaper since she entered Simmons University in 1930, published an article about an open house at a law firm at 744 Hickory Street that had relocated to a building which once housed both Connally Oil Company and Virginia's practice.[4] A distinguishing feature of the building is the 1962 addition of a bomb shelter, popular across America at the time. The *Reporter-News* article told of some treasures housed in the building, including an antique fireplace Ed had brought in from Argentina and woodwork imported from England.

But comments attributed to Virginia were about her favorite possessions, books. The author, Bill Whitaker, wrote, "Dr. Connally recalls stocking the shelter with a Bible 'and all kinds of books you thought you'd want if you knew you were going to be gone a while.'"[5] The same article also displayed a touch of Virginia's wit, which sometimes takes unsuspecting listeners by surprise. According to the article, Virginia remembered the shelter as a mixed blessing: "You didn't know whether you really wanted to go down or not because you thought no one would probably be around when you came out."[6] Over the years, Virginia has shared copies of her beloved *My Utmost for His Highest* and numerous other publications with friends. She is famous for purchasing copies of favorite readings–old and new–to share with friends or even new acquaintances. To this day, Virginia purchases hardback copies of *My Utmost for His Highest* to give to graduating high school seniors at First Baptist Church during the annual baccalaureate service. Not one to complain, her one lament is that even with all the reading she has done over her long life, there is much she will never get to. Nestled among her prayers of thanksgiving for a long, healthy, and fruitful life is one small request of the Almighty. "There is so much more to learn–oh Lord, let me stay a little longer." And when the last day comes, Virginia has plans for carrying on her tradition of sharing her knowledge. In October 2009, the periodical *Baptists Today* profiled Virginia as its cover story. The conclusion of the piece by Executive Editor John D. Pierce gives friends and admirers a hint of what to expect when a final tribute is paid to Virginia: "I've bought a lot of books to be given out at my funeral," she quipped.[7]

In 1929, the year Virginia graduated from high school, she had no idea what her life would hold. But once she was enrolled at Simmons University as a sophomore in 1930, things began to take shape. Carrying on the family's Baptist tradition, she became a member of Abilene's First Baptist Church, embarking on a long life of service to the historic downtown church and the larger Baptist world. On campus, she joined the school's top women's organization, the Cowgirls, whose primary purpose, according to the school's yearbook, *The Bronco*, "was to provide stunts between halves at athletic events."[8] "It's Ex-Cowgirls now," Virginia said with a laugh, "and we're dwindling." For school functions during the years Virginia was a member, the young ladies dressed in boots with cowhide tops, gold jackets, purple skirts and "10-gallon hats" reminiscent of the Western movies popular at the time.[9]

As was the custom, when Virginia was president of the Cowgirls her senior year, she was pictured on the organization's yearbook page dressed in full regalia and sitting atop a rearing horse. The Cowgirls was a forerunner to a tradition the university is now famous for, its Six White Horses program

Virginia as a student at Temple Junior College in 1929.

that has been seen in events across the United States and overseas. Six select young ladies ride the white steeds in parades, each carrying one of the six flags that have flown over Texas. Virginia's younger sister, Francis, attended the university after Virginia and was one of the Six White Horses riders. Virginia also enjoyed other campus social events. A page of photos in her senior yearbook shows young ladies wearing long elegant dresses, apparently ready for a festive occasion. Virginia is pictured in a dark gown, her mid-length hair neatly coiffed. That look was one that Virginia would carry with her throughout her career, believing it important to always dress professionally. Her preferred dress as a professional was a tailored suit, even if it sometimes was partially covered by a white lab coat.

Virginia's extracurricular college activities weren't just in the social realm. Her yearbook entry lists memberships in the Student Association and Science Club, as well as serving as secretary of the Junior Class. Apparently, Virginia was a good note-taker, being elected secretary of each organization she belonged to. Her senior yearbook also noted that Virginia was both a chemistry major and an education major. She would joke later that she decided on medical school to avoid becoming a school teacher. The only stumble Virginia encountered academically came her senior year when she was enrolled in a physics class. Five students were required to make the class and only four had signed up. The professor told Virginia she had to have the class for her pre-med degree plan, when in reality a fifth student was needed to form the class. Virginia had not taken a lower level physics class and knew she wasn't prepared for the senior course. But she enrolled anyway, a decision she would regret. She eventually dropped the course. "It was the only incomplete I ever got," she said, still chagrinned after nearly 80 years. To this day, Virginia isn't sure why she enrolled in the university's pre-med program— other than that she didn't want to be a school teacher. But she has a strong suspicion that Uncle Will's fingerprints were somewhere to be found. "Probably my uncle decided that's the way I should go," she said. "He was an encourager."

Life was casual and uncomplicated on the campus of Simmons University the years Virginia was a student. Ads in *The Bronco* reflect the times. "Good Eats…Reasonable Prices" declared a full-page ad for Simmons Cafeteria, the on-campus eatery.[10] The ad described the dining hall as "A Modern Cafeteria Operated for the Benefit and Service of Simmons Students." The meal plan for fall and spring semesters cost $77.50 each and only $49 for a summer term. *Coca-Cola* was a proud yearbook sponsor, reminding students, "Don't forget to refresh yourself." Page 221 of the 1932 yearbook also carried a full-page ad for West Texas Baptist Sanitarium, "owned and controlled by the Baptists of West Texas." The hospital was the forerunner to today's Hendrick Medical Center, still a Baptist institution. In 1932, E.M. Collier was the superintendent.[11] He still would be in 1940 when Dr. Virginia H. Boyd opened her medical practice in Abilene. In 1960 she would become the hospital's first female chief of staff.

On June 7, 1933, the day Virginia graduated from Simmons University, she was a long way from being Dr. Virginia H. Boyd. But by September, she would be Mrs. Fred Boyd and on her way to becoming "Dr." Boyd. Virginia's life was a whirlwind from June 1933 through her years at LSU School of Medicine and her residency at New Orleans's Charity Hospital. In a span of three months in 1933, she would graduate from college, marry, and travel out of state for the first time in her life to enroll in medical school—something few women did in 1933.

Two of Virginia's aunts, Ada Robertson, left, and Mae Cagle Snow, right, stroll down a sidewalk. Virginia lived with the Snow family while in college in Abilene.

BY LORETTA FULTON

Left to right are Virginia's mother, Stella Hawkins, brother Bartow, who died at age 3, and father Lee Hawkins Sr.

COWGIRLS

VIRGINIA HAWKINS
President

THE Cowgirl organization of Simmons is one typifying the spirit characteristic of this state. It was organized in 1925 by Miss Willie Ray McDonald. The primary purpose was to provide stunts between halves at athletic events.

The uniform is the embodiment of all that the Texas Cowgirl stands for. The original costume consisted of boots with cowhide tops, gold jackets, purple skirts and "ten gallon hats." This year a slight change was made. The jackets were discarded for bright gold satin shirts, and the boots were changed, patterned after regular Cowboy boots. This western regalia makes a very colorful picture as the girls parade. The original stunts of this group have become a much anticipated part of every athletic contest; a stunt is never repeated.

Membership is limited to fifty, and, during recent years, the "freshman" rule has been applied to candidates, thus excluding all first year students. An election and initiation are held once each year, at the beginning of the fall semester. The candidates are entertained for a week before election and there follows a week of initiation activities during which the new members are put through severe drilling tests.

The outstanding event of rush week this year was an Italian supper at the University Cafeteria. The social activities for the week culminated in a beautifully arranged breakfast at the Wooten Hotel. The Annual Homecoming heads all other

Top row: Hawkins, Dillingham, V. Smith, Robertson, Christopher, Wofford, Leck, Ferguson, Benne, Jackson. Bottom row: Worthy, Horton, Green, McGowan, Stokes, Low, McCreary, Melton, Moore, Terry.

Page 94

As president of the Cowgirls her senior year at Simmons University,
Virginia was pictured atop a rearing horse.

BY LORETTA FULTON

Chapter 2
MAKING ADJUSTMENTS

"Only one of you is going to get through."
∽ Medical school professor to
Virginia and her two female classmates

Fred Boyd, two years older than Virginia, was a student at McMurry College, located across town from Simmons University. He had a job as a driver for Virginia's uncle, Dr. Snow, and eventually met Virginia, who worked in her uncle's office answering the telephone. Fred, "nice-looking, well-dressed, neat, and polite," and Virginia eventually got to know each other better. Virginia hadn't dated much and was shy. It took awhile for a relationship to develop, but it did and eventually they decided to get married. September 3, 1933, was the date they chose to be wed in Virginia's parents' home in Temple. "In retrospect, I suspect Uncle Will was putting all this together," Virginia said. "He was quite an arranger." Virginia spent the summer following graduation working in her uncle's office and making wedding plans.

Less than two weeks following the wedding, the couple was on a bus, with no air conditioning, to New Orleans, where both had been accepted at the Louisiana State University School of Medicine. That unpleasant trip was just the beginning of a long journey that didn't always go well. From the beginning, Virginia's will and determination were tested. The couple set up house in an apartment on Canal Street, about ten blocks from the medical school, and Virginia had to learn a lot in a hurry. "I cried for a week," she said. "I had never even kept house." She had not learned to plan and carry out an entire meal. Making candy for Christmas was the only cooking experience she had. When Fred's parents came for a visit, Virginia was determined to prove to the in-laws that she could cook for her husband. She decided on pinto beans for dinner but had never cooked them and had no idea how much to prepare for four people. She greatly overestimated: "We practically had beans coming out the front door!" she said. "I seemed to think I could do everything, but it didn't turn out that way."

Virginia had led a sheltered life, first with her family in Temple and then with her aunt and uncle in Abilene. She had much to adjust to as a newlywed and pioneering female medical student in New Orleans. Just the shock of living in a city so different from what she had known was a daily challenge. "Everything was so different. I had only lived in Temple and Abilene and then to go over there where everyone was speaking a foreign language and eating different foods." A lack of air conditioning in most New Orleans's buildings made the hot, muggy weather even more unbearable. And, the apartment Virginia and Fred shared over a drugstore wasn't the finest. She still recalls the cheap mattress that tended to slope toward the middle, making for sleepless nights. One of her more vivid memories to this day is of the insect population that thrived in the swampy climate in New Orleans. "It wasn't a very good place to live," Virginia said of the apartment, "because it was infested with roaches that were the size of butterflies. They would swoop down at us from one corner." She recalled that life on campus wasn't a whole lot better. The medical school was new, but conditions of the times made sitting through lectures sometimes difficult. Typically, the classroom would have one fan, and it would be trained on the speaker, Virginia recalled. Worse, many students smoked in the classrooms, with no windows open. With no air conditioning and no breeze circulating, Virginia remembered oftentimes trying to listen to the professor with tears streaming down her face. Virginia and Fred had little money and no car, so escaping the routine of school and the uncomfortable living conditions was difficult. The only time they visited the city's famed French Quarter was when someone came to see them and took them out for a night on the town.

Even with a tiring daily grind, Virginia never considered

LSU School of Medicine – original façade, before expansion

sleeping in on a Sunday morning. She found a Baptist church on Napoleon Avenue and took the streetcar to services. "Sometimes I would go to sleep before we would get there," she remembered. Occasionally the couple would take in a movie, if time and money allowed. But even there, sleep took precedence. Virginia remembered going to see *Gone With the*

Wind, only to nod off periodically. "When I would wake up, I felt like I hadn't missed a thing, it was so long," she said. From what she did see, she wasn't impressed but liked Clark Gable so much that the experience was worthwhile. To this day, she still hasn't seen *Gone With the Wind* in its entirety.

But most of Fred and Virginia's time was spent either in class or studying. After one year at the LSU School of Medicine, Fred decided to become a dentist, and transferred to Loyola University, five miles west of the LSU School of Medicine. After only one year of marriage, Fred and Virginia were living separately, which in retrospect Virginia believes signaled the beginning of the end of the marriage. "So much of the time we were apart. You have to grow together." But before Fred transferred, the two shared experiences in medical school that Virginia still chuckles over. "I remember we worked together on the same cadaver," she said. Beginning med students were told to bring a razor and brush to "clean up" the cadaver before work began in earnest. When Virginia and Fred entered the LSU School of Medicine in September 1933, the school was barely two years old. In fact, the first graduates of the school, including women, earned their diplomas in 1933. Those graduates were junior transfers from two-year schools, most notably from Alabama, according to Dr. Russell C. Klein, MD, and LSU Health Sciences Center Director of Special Projects, who wrote *A History of LSU School of Medicine-New Orleans*.[1] According to Klein's research, the first class, which entered October 1, 1931, included one woman, Virginia Webb of Alabama.[2]

McMurry College in Abilene was a four-year school, but Fred apparently was allowed to transfer to the LSU School of Medicine while still an undergraduate, just like transfers who had completed two-year schools. The McMurry Registrar's Office records show that Fred was enrolled in 1932 but not 1933. The records do not indicate that he graduated from McMurry. Nevertheless, he apparently was a bright student, graduating with a DDS degree on June 5, 1939, in the top quarter of his class at Loyola.[3] With Fred moving

BY LORETTA FULTON

to a separate apartment, Virginia moved into a dormitory-type space for female students over the ambulance bay on the Charity Hospital grounds. She was allowed to stay away from the hospital one night a month and, of course, spent that time at Fred's apartment. She remembered one eventful stay when a fire broke out in the house where Fred rented an apartment. She had just bathed and washed her long, blond hair. "I remember picking up my gold hairpins and getting out of there!" she said.

One reason Virginia chose the LSU School of Medicine was because of its infancy. It was one of the few that would accept women. Virginia believes the out-of-state tuition, $500 at the time, was another reason the university so gladly welcomed a diversity of students. The school dates its beginning to January 3, 1931, when members of the LSU Board of Supervisors and the New Orleans Charity Hospital Governing Board were summoned to the hotel suite of Governor Huey Long, according to Klein's research from *A History of LSU School of Medicine-New Orleans*.[4]

He (Long) proposed the establishment of a School of Medicine in New Orleans and that (Dr. Arthur Vidrine, Sr.) continue both as Superintendent of Charity Hospital, and serve also as its Dean.

With little discussion, Huey's proposals were adopted. The School was born. Huey needed a site and the Charity Board obligingly donated vacant land in the 1500 block of Tulane Avenue."[5]

According to Klein's book, a newspaper accused Long of stealing a million dollars from the Highway Trust Fund to pay for construction. Long indignantly retorted that he had stolen two million dollars and to, "publish what you want but we will have a medical school for the poor boys of Louisiana."[6] Long, a flamboyant politician nicknamed the Kingfish, served as governor from 1928 to 1932 and as a U.S. Senator from 1932 to 1935, when he was assassinated. He was shot September 8, 1935, at the Louisiana State Capitol in Baton Rouge and died two days later. Virginia remembered hearing of Long's death while she was on a train headed back to Texas for a visit.

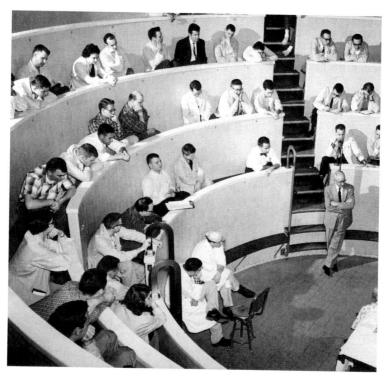

LSU School of Medicine Amphitheater --
James D. Rives, MD, in the pit

Long may have had Louisiana's "poor boys" in mind when he dreamed of a medical school in New Orleans, but the school also opened its doors to women, a rarity in those days. Only three women were in Virginia's class when she entered in 1933–Ellanor Lockhart, Viola Dickson Nelken, and Virginia. Lockhart and Nelken are both deceased. Even though women were admitted to the school, they were not always welcomed or treated as equals to the male students. Virginia recalled a professor stepping into an elevator one day with the three female classmates. "Only one of you is going to get through," was his prediction for their success rate. They proved him wrong and all three graduated.

Klein also noted in his book the difficulty women students of the time had in medical school. Female students

BY LORETTA FULTON

in the early-to mid-1930s were required to attend a lecture on adapting to work in a traditionally male environment. The lecturer, a woman, reminded the female students not to lose their femininity. [7] Other speakers were less kind, Klein noted:

> During a talk in New Orleans in the mid-1930s, Morris Fishbein, president of the American Medical Association, a man described as having a lightning rod for a personality, rebuked the presence of women in the American medical workforce. He contended that women had no place in medicine and ridiculed them for spending too much money on cosmetics, saying that a look at his audience would prove his point. [8]

Klein wrote that the stigma against women in medicine would continue for decades. But, he praised those trailblazing women who "provided a benchmark of achievement for those who followed." At present, Klein noted, women make up nearly 50 percent of new LSU medical school classes. [9]

Virginia certainly could vouch for Klein's observation that female students at the time "felt the effects of discrimination and criticism most acutely." She recalled the same professor who delighted in trying to intimidate her and two other female students on the elevator also made life difficult in the classroom. A urologist, the professor had the female students recite terms of the male anatomy aloud in class in an effort to embarrass them. They also became quite familiar with the intricacies of performing rectal examinations, Virginia remembered. Outside the classroom, life wasn't much better for the female students. If a woman walked into the dining room alone, the men would stop eating and begin banging a spoon or fork against a glass. "They were just calling attention to see how embarrassed we would be," Virginia recalled. But by the time the female students reached the internship and residency stages of their education, they were treated better by the males who were "glad to share the work."

Even though the LSU School of Medicine was new, it offered an excellent education with top professors. According to Klein's book, *A History of LSU School of Medicine-New Orleans*, medical students followed a traditional course of study. Basic science classes taught the first two years included anatomy, pharmacology, physiology, biochemistry, bacteriology and pathology. The final two years were devoted to clinical instruction. [10] Klein noted that the medical school counted "many giants" in the field among its staff:

> George Sam Bel, a renowned internist and former president of the Louisiana State Medical Society, was a professor of Internal Medicine and served as Departmental Chair succeeding Dr. J. Bernie Guthrie. He was also on the Charity Hospital Board and a close friend of Arthur Vidrine. Richard Ashman was recruited from Vanderbilt by Clyde Brooks, first chairman of the combined Department of Pharmacology and Physiology, as a faculty member in Physiology. Ashman's work in electrocardiography would forever change the way doctors looked a diagnosing heart disease. In 1932 the combined department would be separated, Brooks retaining the chairmanship of Pharmacology and Ashman becoming Head of Physiology and Director of the Charity Hospital Heart Station. [11]

Faculty members were making a name for themselves during the years Virginia was a student. In 1936, Dr. Rigney D'Aunoy, chairman and professor in the combined Department of Pathology and Bacteriology and associate dean of the School of Medicine, along with Emmerich von Hamm, were recognized by the American Society of Clinical Pathologists with a Gold Medal for their research on the cause of granuloma inguinale, a sexually transmitted disease. [12] In 1937, D'Aunoy became dean of the medical school but served only two years and was replaced by Beryl I. Burns. Klein noted that the move was welcomed in the medical school. D'Aunoy was a competent physician but a harsh taskmaster and was feared by faculty and students, Klein wrote. [13]

Also during those years, a young physician named Michael E. DeBakey was becoming well known. Born September 7, 1908, in Lake Charles, Louisiana, DeBakey earned bachelor's, master's, and medical degrees from Tulane University in New Orleans. DeBakey completed his internship and residency in surgery at Charity Hospital. Virginia recalled that even though DeBakey was just four years her senior, he would come to the LSU School of Medicine periodically to teach classes.

34

He later became famous world-wide for his research that led to development of an artificial heart. In 1966, DeBakey performed the first successful implanting into a human of a partial artificial heart that he devised–a left ventricular assist device.[14] Before his death July 11, 2008, DeBakey would be known the world over as, a "true Renaissance man, with interests and knowledge ranging across a broad spectrum of disciplines beyond medicine, including history, philosophy, ethics, literature, art, and music, as well as socioeconomic and cultural fields of study."[15]

DeBakey's brilliance was well-noted long before *Time* magazine put him on the cover of its May 28, 1965, edition. He also was cited in *Time Books' Great Events of the Twentieth Century* in 1999, as well as numerous other national and international publications for his exemplary achievements. From 1937 to 1948, DeBakey was a faculty member of the Tulane School of Medicine Department of Surgery. Virginia recalled a lecture DeBakey gave at LSU while still in his 20s. The future pioneer in heart transplant surgery demonstrated a new type of transfusion "that was just a marvel to everybody," Virginia recalled. "He was a brain and everybody recognized it."

Despite the knowledge and experience she was gaining, the trials of attending medical school, combined with a less-than-perfect life off-campus, were at times almost more than Virginia could bear. But she was blessed with an abundance of determination, a solid faith, and a brilliant mind. She also understood the reality that quitting might have been tougher than staying. "In those days, it was sort of a one-way ticket," she said. "I didn't want to walk back to Texas." To make matters worse, Virginia had not aspired to be a doctor. In fact, she hadn't even thought of it until her uncle began guiding her in that direction. Another reality also influenced her. In 1933, when Virginia graduated from Simmons University, women were limited in their choices of professional careers. Becoming a doctor usually wasn't among those choices, and for Virginia it was more attractive than what she thought was her only other choice, becoming a school teacher. The latter was not an option for Virginia. As an undergraduate taking education courses she was required to do student teaching. Whether true or not, Virginia viewed that experience as a failure, acknowledging that, "Whatever they learned they would have learned just as well without me."

All those factors–determination, faith, keen intellect, and limited alternatives–would come into play by the time Virginia reached her third year of medical school. She recalled taking exams every day that year, plus three on Saturday. The rigors of the academic and clinical training at one point made her declare in frustration, "I don't care whether I pass or not–just let me out of here!" But she did pass, stuck it out, and earned her degree in 1937. Three years later, as medicine gradually became a calling for Virginia, not just a career choice, she would begin her practice in treating diseases of the eye, ear, nose, and throat in Abilene. In a strange coincidence in the history of medicine in Abilene, so did another doctor, J.D. Magee Jr.

The parallels between the two are remarkable. Magee was born in Abilene on July 29, 1910. His father, Dr. J.D. Magee Sr., was one of the charter members of the Taylor County Medical Society, which was authorized on April 26, 1904, by the Texas Medical Association.[16] The elder Magee, a physician and surgeon, was the father of five sons and all went into the field of medicine. Magee Jr. graduated from Simmons University, as did Virginia, in 1930 and was enrolled in the Tulane University School of Medicine from 1930 to 1932. He graduated from the Louisiana State University School of Medicine in 1934 with a doctor of medicine degree.[17] Magee served an internship and residency at Charity Hospital from July 1, 1934, to July 1, 1936. He studied obstetrics from 1936 to 1937 and ophthalmology and otolaryngology from 1938 to 1940 at LSU School of Medicine and Charity Hospital. Unlike Virginia, Magee graduated from the School of Aviation Medicine at Randolph Field in San Antonio in 1939, which would prove significant when he was called to active duty in the Medical Reserve Corps of the U.S. Army Air Corps on

May 28, 1941. After stints at several military installations in the United States, Magee eventually spent time in New Guinea and the Philippines. He finished his service as a lieutenant colonel and resumed his practice in Abilene in 1946.[18]

Virginia knew Magee when they were both students in New Orleans, and they were friends. But limited time, money, and transportation didn't leave much time for socializing. Once they were finished with their schooling, both returned to Abilene in 1940 and began treating diseases of the eye, ear, nose, and throat. Magee died June 12, 1988, at age 77.[19] Virginia and Magee shared a few career posts during their years in practice. Both served as president of the Taylor-Jones County Medical Society (now the Taylor-Jones-Haskell-Callahan County Medical Society). Virginia was president in 1949 and Magee was elected in 1960. Both were chief of staff at Hendrick Medical Center, Magee serving in 1959 and Virginia elected in December 1960 to serve in 1961. Both were members of the Texas Medical Association and the American Medical Association. However, in 1940 when both returned to Abilene to treat diseases of the eye, ear, nose, and throat, the landscape was a little different for Virginia–the first woman to announce she was opening an office to practice medicine.

Virginia receives the Distinguished Alumna Award from
Hardin-Simmons University in 1973

BY LORETTA FULTON

Chapter 3

STEPPING INTO HISTORY -
IN HIGH HEELS

"Our day will come; we will work in faith and bide our time."
∞ Ann Preston, dean of the Female Medical College
of Pennsylvania, to the Class of 1855-1856

In 1988, the YWCA and the *Abilene Reporter-News* sponsored a reception for the first 24 recipients of a new award called Pathfinders. The inaugural award, and future ones, would honor "distinguished women who have forged new trails for all women to follow," according to an account in the October 30, 1988, issue of the local newspaper.[1] The presenter at the program, held in the historic Paramount Theatre in downtown Abilene, was Mary Scott Nabers, a pathfinder herself who was serving as the first woman appointed to a six-year term on the Texas Employment Commission.[2] Among the recipients was Virginia, who had retired six years earlier after a 42-year medical career. Twenty-one years later, Virginia would be the first recipient of another "pathfinder award," the Legacy Award presented by the Abilene Woman's Club, which Virginia joined in 1955. Virginia rightfully has been honored as a "pathfinder," "pioneer," and "trailblazer" in her lifetime, but she also is quick to note that she benefitted from others who blazed trails before her.

In the medical field, two of those trailblazers would be Elizabeth Blackwell, who in 1849 became the first female to earn a medical degree from a medical school in the United States,[3] and Marie Delalondre Dietzel, the first woman to graduate from the University of Texas Medical Branch, earning a degree in 1897, according to Elizabeth Silverthorne in her book, *Women Pioneers in Texas Medicine*.[4] After graduating in 1849 from New York's Geneva Medical College, Blackwell supported other women wanting to study medicine by founding, with colleagues, the New York Infirmary for Women and Children in 1857. She also published several important books on the issue of women in medicine, including *Medicine as a Profession For Women* in 1860 and *Address on the Medical Education of Women* in 1864.

Dietzel earned her degree from the University of Texas Medical Branch in 1897, one year after the university's president, Dr. Leslie Waggener, publicly proclaimed his opposition to women in medicine, although women were not officially denied admission to the school.[5] Silverthorne recorded Waggener's remarks on the topic in his last public address, delivered in Austin in May 1896, at the Texas Woman's Press Association:

I understand that many young women are looking forward to studying medicine as a profession and that already there is hardly a large city, even in the South, in which there are not one or two female doctors. Against these personally I have not a word to say. But I deplore the effect of the example they set. The work of a doctor or surgeon is not work for a woman.[6]

According to Silverthorne's book, Waggener died later that year, missing out on Dietzel's graduation by a year. When the dean of the Medical Branch, Dr. J.F.Y. Paine, reported on the feat to the Board of Regents on May 15, 1897, his tone was markedly different from the late president's:

While women have been admitted on equal terms with men to all the lectures and other exercises of both schools, medicine and pharmacy, since the organization of the medical department, it is worthy of mention that this is the first occasion on which they have been recommended for degrees. It is a source of gratification that the young lady made notable in the history of the college by being the first lady of her sex to secure a degree in medicine is a modest and gentle lady, yet brave and independent.[7]

Silverthorne noted that Dietzel "had met the challenge and fulfilled the promise" made by Ann Preston to the Class of 1855-56 at the Female Medical College of Pennsylvania, the first chartered medical school for women in the world, which opened in Philadelphia in 1850. In 1855-1856 Preston was dean of the school, which Virginia later would serve as a board member, when she made her "promise" that "Our day will come; we will work in faith and bide our time."[8]

Of course, before any women carried the initials "M.D." after their names, other women were practicing medicine, primarily as nurses or midwives. Authors Sylvia Van Voast Ferris and Eleanor Sellers Hoppe both of Abilene traced the history of some of these women and the institutions that were formed to support training for women in their book, *Scalpels and Sabers: Nineteenth Century Medicine in Texas.* Hoppe's father, Dr. Erle D. Sellers, came to Abilene in 1926 to practice medicine. Hoppe said she "toyed with the idea" of becoming a doctor, herself, but soon discovered she loved literature more than the study of medicine. She recalled that her father was impressed with Virginia's achievement, which paved the way for more women to practice medicine. "He was real proud of her," Hoppe recalled.

The first formal institution to train women as nurses in Texas was established in 1890 and called the Training School for Nurses. Organized by women in Galveston, the school was associated with the John Sealy Hospital. When the school was affiliated with the University of Texas in 1897, it became the John Sealy School of Nursing.[9] Known today as the University of Texas Medical Branch School of Nursing, it was the first such school west of the Mississippi when it opened March 10, 1890.[10]

Ferris and Hoppe recorded short histories of several women who were among the state's first women physicians, practicing in the late 19th and early 20th centuries. But it wasn't until 1940 that a licensed woman physician hung out her shingle in Abilene. The small notice about the establishment of Virginia's practice in the *Abilene Reporter-News* didn't really do justice to the significance of that achievement. Years later, Virginia would come to be honored as the pioneer she was, but when she opened an office with "Virginia H. Boyd, M.D."

on the door in 1940, little note was paid. The newspapers, including *the Abilene Reporter-News*, were filled with news of the war raging overseas. The front pages of the *Reporter-News* in 1940 carried headlines such as, "Nazi, Italian Troops Mass Along Coast," "and "Embargo Seen As Axis Blow." The latter sounded an ominous warning:

> The spokesperson for the Japanese admiralty described President Roosevelt's ban on exporting aviation gasoline from the western hemisphere as an act directed against Japan and the Rome-Berlin Axis.[11]

Local goings-on didn't go unnoticed in those troubling times. "Heat Record for Summer is Equalled (sic)" shared front page space with news of Nazi troops gathering steam. The story reported that the city's highest temperature of the summer, 102 degrees, was equaled the previous day, July 31.[12] On August 3, 1940, the newspaper carried an article letting readers know what they probably already suspected, "Past Month Driest in Abilene History." The story reported that in the 55-year history of the Weather Bureau, no month had been drier than July 1940, when .12 of an inch of rain fell, leaving the city 3.8 inches below normal for the year. On most days, foreboding headlines from distant lands incongruously shared front page space with less world-shaking news. The headline, "German Bombs Threaten London," blared across the top of the front page of the morning edition on Wednesday, August 14, 1940. Taking up a smaller space at the bottom of the front page was a story titled, "First 1940 Bale Ginned at Rotan." The bale weighed in at 487 pounds.[13]

A front page article on Saturday, August 3, 1940, carried the intriguing headline, "Ordinance Won't Cover As Much As Shorts." The story was illustrated with two drawings, one depicting a sharp-nosed elderly woman wearing an ankle-length skirt, long-sleeved blouse and carrying an umbrella that she appeared poised to use as a weapon. The other drawing showed a younger, scantily clad lass with an obviously more pleasing disposition. The lead of the story summed up the dilemma at hand:

The Abilene city commission was presented Friday afternoon with a petition asking restriction of wearing of shorts on the streets but consensus of the members was that there is little they can do about such things.[14]

The story went on to report that a citizen had handed the commission petitions signed by 1,212 people requesting an ordinance be enacted prohibiting the wearing of shorts by car hops or other women on public streets. Mayor Will W. Hair had seen the storm clouds forming and came to the meeting prepared with two state laws regulating "indecent exposure of the person." He reported that he did not believe the city commission had the power to prescribe the way women or men could dress. The woman who presented the petitions remarked that she understood that Galveston had an ordinance "prohibiting the appearance on streets of women in bathing suits." To which City Attorney E.M. Overshiner replied, "Last time I was in Galveston there were plenty of women on the streets in bathing suits."[15]

Inside the newspaper, popular comics such as Red Ryder, Dick Tracy, and Superman provided brief escapes from reality.[16] Advertisements enticed readers who could afford it to see Mickey Rooney and Judy Garland in "Andy Hardy Meets Debutante" at the Paramount Theater.[17] The local Safeway grocery store tried to attract shoppers with ads touting Thompson seedless grapes for five cents per pound; lettuce, five cents per head; potatoes, ten pounds for 19 cents; Edwards coffee, 21 cents for a one-pound can; and ham, 14 cents per pound.[18] A competitor, Piggly Wiggly, had its own specials: Gold Chain Flour, six-pound sack, 27 cents; beef steak, fifteen cents per pound; and sliced bologna, nine cents per pound.[19] Other ads were even more enticing: "1941 Plymouths Are In," featuring the latest in driving technology, "Powermatic Shifting." A Camel cigarette ad pictured a man and woman on horseback, extolling virtues of the smokes that promised "EXTRA Mildness, EXTRA Coolness, EXTRA Flavor."[20]

Interestingly, a report in the *Texas State Journal of Medicine* concerning the February 13, 1940, meeting of the Taylor-Jones County Medical Society tells of a program led by Comer Clay, debate coach at Abilene High School. Under Clay's direction, four debaters, including Virginia's aunt, Mae Cagle Snow, entertained the doctors with the pros and cons of "Resolved: That Texas should adopt a system of complete medical service available to all citizens at public expense."[21] The report didn't say which side prevailed, only that two people on each side of the argument debated. Seventy years later, paying for health care still is being debated.

Into that historical picture stepped Dr. Virginia H. Boyd. A few miles outside of Abilene, another historical event also was unfolding. In November 1940, just a couple of months after Virginia opened her office, land was secured near the community of View, southwest of Abilene, for an Army base to be called Camp Barkeley. A headline in the November 26, 1940, issue of the *Abilene Reporter-News* stated simply, "Tent Camp."[22] Eventually it would be home to the 45th and 90th Infantry Divisions and the 11th and 12th Armored Divisions. In May 1942, the Medical Administrative Corps Officer Candidate School was activated at Camp Barkeley and graduated about 12,500 candidates.[23] By the time the base was deactivated on April 30, 1945, it had become much more than a "Tent Camp," housing more than 50,000 men at its peak.[24] According to the 1940 U.S. Census, the population of nearby Abilene was just over half that–26,612. Even though Camp Barkeley was short-lived, it had a lasting effect on Abilene, boosting the local economy, and laying the groundwork for the government's later decision to establish Dyess Air Force Base in Abilene.[25]

The onset of World War II and the establishment of the Army base twice the size of the city proved to play a role in Virginia's early years in practice. Male physicians were going off to war, making Virginia's acceptance easier. "So many of them were leaving, and they were glad to see me," she said. And, soldiers needing care provided by an eye, ear, nose, and throat specialist were counted among Virginia's earliest patients as she began to establish a clientele. "It seemed like I never lacked for patients," Virginia recalled. "I worked from dark to dark." On at least one occasion, a uniformed soldier even served as an impromptu bodyguard for Virginia. Never one to say "no," Virginia agreed to make an office call late one night. When she arrived at her downtown office in the Mims Building, a group of soldiers had congregated on the street. She was alone and her office was on the eighth floor. A little apprehensive about being trapped upstairs with someone she didn't know, Virginia chose to enlist the aid of a young soldier. "I just grabbed one of them and said, 'I have to go up to see a patient—would you go with me?' He did."

The Mims Building, where Virginia first opened her practice, was constructed in 1926 at 1049 North Third Street, on the corner of Cypress and North Third streets in the heart of the city. The 1941 *Abilene City Directory* listed Virginia's name for the first time: "Boyd, Virginia H., Mrs. phys 813 Mims Building r Abilene State Hospital."[26] Fred was employed as a dentist at Abilene State Hospital, and that's where the couple lived after returning from New Orleans. The facility became the Abilene State School and in 2009 was renamed the Abilene State Supported Living Center. Fred was listed separately in the 1941 city directory, with "Virginia" in parentheses as his wife.[27] The Mims Building, which today houses BBVA Compass Bank as its main occupant, originally was home to a conglomerate of interests. Probably best known was the dry goods store on the ground floor. Upstairs offices housed professionals such as Virginia, whose office was on the top floor, and an early-day philanthropist, oilman, rancher, and former county and district judge in nearby Stephens County, Clifton Mott Caldwell.[28] Among his numerous achievements and acts of generosity, Caldwell donated land for what is now Hendrick Medical Center, where Virginia performed untold numbers of tonsillectomies and served as chief of staff in 1961. Caldwell served for many years as chairman of the board of trustees of what is now Hardin-Simmons University, Virginia's alma mater.[29]

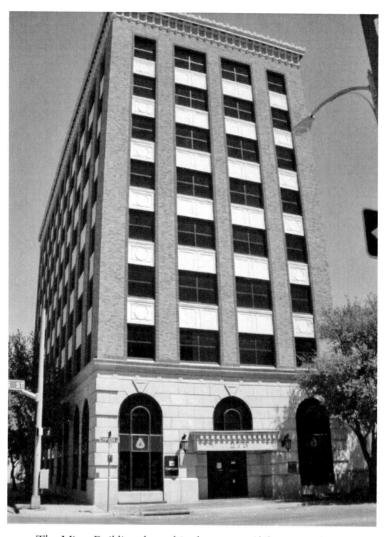

The Mims Building, located in downtown Abilene, was the site of Virginia's original office.

Virginia remembers well the acts of kindness that Caldwell was noted for. She recalled that on Saturdays he would stroll the eighth-floor hallway handing out dimes to patients waiting to be seen. The Mims Building has been renovated numerous times over the years, but a recent tour prompted recollections of those long-ago days when Virginia,

BY LORETTA FULTON

Caldwell, and many other Abilene stalwarts occupied the building. "The elevator must have been over there," Virginia said as she walked the hallway where patients once waited. "It's changed–like I have." Although she doesn't remember much about the type of equipment she used during those early days of her practice, Virginia does recall one important aspect of those years. She was able to put together enough money to pay for the equipment and a car "just like clockwork." That achievement was especially significant to Virginia because, she recalled, she had never even so much as applied for a job prior to opening her own practice. That meant learning the ins and outs of running a business in addition to establishing a new medical practice as the first female physician in town. Determined as always, Virginia set about mastering the art of running a business. "I just learned it as I went along," she said.

A tour of the Mims Building also prompted memories of living in the nearby Wooten Hotel for several years during Virginia's early years in practice after Fred had left for service in the Army. The 1944 *Abilene City Directory* lists the Wooten as her home, and that also was the year that her only daughter, Genna, was born in Temple, where Virginia's parents lived. Touring the Mims Building, Virginia peered out the window of the eighth-floor office that once housed her practice. "We lived right over there," she said, pointing to the landmark downtown hotel catty-corner across the intersection. She and Genna lived on the sixth floor, and Virginia recalled a distinct feature of their dwelling. "I remember it was decorated with roses of different sizes," she said. She also recalled that West Texas Utilities was located across the street and provided Genna with her first word, "light." Another, not so pleasant memory, involved late-night fire calls. Virginia could hear the fire engines roar up to the building, even with no sirens blaring. It was a frequent occurrence. "People would just drop cigarettes in the laundry chute," Virginia recalled. "I developed a real fear of fire," perhaps remembering the blaze that sent her fleeing from Fred's apartment in New Orleans when they were students.

Chapter 4
EARNING HER STRIPES

"They said they would let me know if they needed me, but I never heard from them."
∞ Virginia Connally on volunteering
for service in World War II

With an Army base filled with soldiers and male physicians leaving for military service, it didn't take Virginia long to start building a patient base. In fact, she saw her first patient before even opening her office. A local pharmacist called and asked her if she would treat a woman who accidentally had put iodine drops in her eyes. Virginia obliged, and her long career in medicine in Abilene had officially started. In those early days, reception from male physicians and from patients varied from one day to the next. An attitude that only men were suited for the practice of medicine still prevailed among much of the populace. The federal government had a definite opinion. Nurses were highly sought after to serve in the military with war looming, but female physicians were another matter. Virginia remembered that practically every physician in town volunteered for military service, even though not all actually served. Virginia did her duty, too, volunteering to serve alongside the male physicians. "I was commended for volunteering," she recalled. "They said they would let me know if they needed me, but I never heard from them."

Some local residents had the same attitude about women doctors. Early on, Virginia was one of only two doctors in town who specialized in diseases of the eye, ear, nose, and throat. So she got her fair share of patients with cataracts, sinus infections, tonsillitis, or just in need of new glasses. She recalled realizing that she had actually "made it" into the male world of medicine when people started calling her "doctor."

And if they didn't, she didn't like it. A soldier from Camp Barkeley came into her office one day seeking relief from a sinus infection. He made the mistake of calling her "Virginia" instead of "Dr. Boyd." He left with the sinus infection still raging and–perhaps–his ears ringing. Virginia immediately dismissed the impertinent young man, mincing no words: "You don't come back. You get someone else to treat you."

Virginia remembered another incident early in her practice–in the days when physicians made house calls. A woman called for an appointment, apparently not realizing the name "Virginia" was feminine. "I walked up with my case and she looked at me and scowled," Virginia remembered. "She was NOT going to have a woman doctor. I went and got right back in my car and drove off." She was greeted by similar disrespect from a few physicians, including a medical school classmate who established a practice in a nearby community about the same time Virginia opened her office in Abilene. The doctor had a tonsillectomy patient who was experiencing bleeding that the doctor was unable to stop. So, he sent the patient to Virginia, knowing that tonsillectomies were her specialty. She cured the young patient and sent the bill to the county where the physician practiced, as he had instructed. "He was furious because I sent a bill," Virginia said. The county treasurer balked at the bill and in the end nobody paid Virginia for her service.

Despite negative reactions from a few patients–and condescension from some doctors–Virginia's name and reputation spread. Longtime friend and admirer, Laura Thaxton of Abilene, recalled that when she was a freshman and sophomore at Anson High School in the 1940s, her family went to Virginia for eye, ear, nose, and throat ailments. Laura's father, Dr. J.P. (Phinis) McBeth, was pastor of First Baptist Church in Anson and that may be the reason he knew of Virginia, Laura said. The family all liked and respected Virginia and continued to see her professionally after moving to Sweetwater. When Laura graduated from high school in Sweetwater, she enrolled at Hardin-Simmons. During her junior and senior years, she was a member of the Cowgirls organization, the same one Virginia served as president her senior year. Today, Thaxton is the Ex-Cowgirls historian and helps organize the group's twice-a-year gatherings, faithfully attended by Virginia. In 1952, a year after graduating from Hardin-Simmons, Thaxton married Warren Thaxton, also a Hardin-Simmons graduate. Not long afterward, Laura had a problem with her tonsils, a recurring issue since childhood. "Dr. Virginia," as Laura called her, recommended a tonsillectomy, to be performed at the now-shuttered St. Ann Hospital. Afterward, when the Thaxtons went to Virginia to pay the bill, Virginia asked Warren, "Would you like me to send this bill to her daddy—this should have been done years ago!"

In those years, most of Virginia's practice was conducted from her office, but she still made some house calls, despite being rebuffed by occasional unsuspecting patients. Her daughter, Genna, often accompanied her mother on hospital rounds and house calls when she was a child. She still remembers the "last straw" for Virginia. "Mother told me to stay in the car and lock it. She went up some unpainted steps and through the screen door of a two-story older house, calling on an elderly woman who was having eye pain. She wasn't there long. She told me as we drove away hurriedly that she would never make another house call and that the family frightened her with their rudeness." Genna still recalls being upset because she saw something in Virginia that she rarely saw. Her mother was scared.

The house calls ended, but Virginia's practice grew. The 1946 *Abilene City Directory* showed both Fred and Virginia with offices on the second floor of the Medical Building, 1052 North Fifth Street. Their residence was listed at 1702 Belmont Boulevard.[1] Genna remembered pleasant times in the home, including the fresh smells of the wash hanging on the line that faced a side street and the sound of the starch bottle being shaken by the housekeeper who did the ironing in the kitchen. She also recalled the sound of "steam escaping from the new sit-down ironing machine and light, summer wind blowing the transparent white curtains in my bedroom windows where I played every chance I had with a two-story wooden dollhouse." Virginia also took her young daughter to the hospital with her, sometimes leaving her in the locked car in the doctors' parking lot with the radio on so Genna could listen to the latest episode of *The Lone Ranger*. One time, Genna fell asleep in the car and Virginia had to summon passersby to help her wake Genna to open the door.

Other times, Genna would make the rounds with her mother. She and her mother usually took the stairs at Hendrick Memorial Hospital, but Genna remembers on occasion hopping into the cage elevator beside her mother. A red and yellow popcorn machine greeted them on the third floor. The two would share a small bag and then get shaved ice from a machine near the operating room. Genna recalls the emergency room nurses bragging that they raised her and watched over her as she slept on a gurney outside the ER when her mother was on call. As Genna matured, Virginia allowed her to assist by holding a magnifying lens or by handing her a solution she used to wash out an eye. "She could turn the eyelid inside out with one flick of her finger," Genna still marvels. "I remember her always finding the minute steel particles a welder had managed to get into his eye. I felt proud to be part of her team."

Over the years, Genna got so used to accompanying her mother that she could even discern Virginia's footsteps on the black-and-white stone hospital floors. Virginia always wore heels, and they made a distinctive click-clack sound. "She almost danced everywhere she went," Genna recalled. "She walked as quickly as her mind raced."

Just as children no longer assist their physician parent in the emergency room, many other aspects of medicine have changed dramatically since Virginia started practicing in 1940. Today's medical journals barely resemble the publications of the 1940s. No longer does Philip Morris tout the superiority of its cigarettes such as in ads on facing pages in the July 1942

Texas State Journal of Medicine. One page stated:

> The published studies on cigarette differences are merely a starting point. It is only when doctors make their *own* tests…on their *own* patients who smoke…that they are fully convinced of Philip Morris superiority. That is why we suggest that *you* try Philip Morris on *your* patients. Your findings will confirm the published studies which showed that: On changing to Philip Morris cigarettes, every case of irritation of the nose and throat due to smoking cleared completely or definitely improved.[2]

The facing page led with the headline, "Cigarette information worth knowing," followed by the statement, "Philip Morris do (sic) not claim to cure irritation but they do say this: 62.3 percent of the cases of irritation of the nose and throat due to smoking cleared completely on changing to Philip Morris (and) 37.7 percent, the balance, showed definite improvement."[3] Other advertisements touted the latest in medicines and medical technology. The Gilbert X-Ray Company of Dallas advertised, "Medicine moves forward with X-Ray." The ad showed a science fiction-looking gizmo being used on a patient. The text stated that the name of "Waite" had played a role in the development and perfection of X-ray apparatus. "Waite gave to the world of X-ray its *first* completely shockproof units, its *first* Oil Immersed Valve Tubes, its *first* Flexible Shockproof Therapy Equipment and its *first* Automatic Safety Controls."[4]

A brief report from the Taylor-Jones County Medical Society meeting of February 11, 1947, showed how far medicine had yet to go in fighting illnesses that are easily treated in the twenty-first century. Dr. W.B. Adamson reported to the society on rheumatic fever, still a deadly disease in 1947. Adamson emphasized "the care which must be exercised in using orthodox methods of treatment so that the patient will not on the one hand come to consider himself an invalid and sink into a psychopathic mental state and on the other hand will not believe himself so healthy that he harms himself." In a discussion that followed Adamson's presentation, according to the report, "several physicians recommended occupational therapy as a means to prevent undue anxiety on the part of the patient."[5]

In those days, when Virginia wasn't working or tending to Genna, she stayed on top of all the latest medical developments–even, as Genna recalled, reading from the *Journal of the American Medical Association* to lull her daughter to sleep. With Virginia's husband away for a year at Northwestern University to study orthodontia, and later in California as an Army dentist, Virginia was left to take care of herself and Genna. Those long separations took their toll on Virginia and Fred's marriage. "He was a different person when he came home, and so was I," Virginia said. "I was practicing medicine by then. He was issuing orders." Virginia was used to giving orders, not taking them, and the marriage ended in 1948. The divorce meant that Virginia would step into another unusual world for women at the time–that of divorcee and single parent. As usual, she never skipped a beat. She was determined as always to do her best in both medicine and in parenthood.

Virginia, right, hugs her sister "Babe" Ruth.

BY LORETTA FULTON

Chapter 5
CHARTING A COURSE

"She gets five stars from me."
   ❊ Boone Powell, Jr., retired administrator,
Hendrick Medical Center

The year 1948 was a major one in Virginia's life. It was marked by both a personal setback due to a failed marriage and by a huge step forward professionally. In eight years, she had grown a large practice and had earned the respect and admiration of male peers. As a sign of just how much of an impression she had on fellow physicians, Virginia was elected president of the Taylor-Jones County Medical Society on November 9, 1948. Again, the big news carried only a small headline atop a brief, one-column story in the November 10, 1948, morning issue of the *Abilene Reporter-News*: "Virginia Boyd Heads Medics."[1]

Just as Virginia's election as head of the medical society was an indicator of the progress being made for women in the world of medicine, another brief report in the local newspaper the following March showed how far women still had to go in being recognized for more than their looks. The Sunday, March 20, 1949, cover of the "Social, Editorials, Features Section" of the *Abilene Reporter-News* carried a large photo of Virginia, along with four other women. The heading read, "Abilene Women Take the West Texas Spotlight."[2] The caption under Virginia's photo noted that she was "serving as the first woman ever elected president of the local medical society," and was "an attractive blonde." Indeed, her photo backed up that assertion.

She also was an esteemed physician and a proud mother. The late-1940s were a time of bonding for Genna and Virginia, good times that still hold fond memories for both. Trips to the grandparents' farm at Temple were especially memorable

---

for Genna. Favorite travel foods were *Coca-Cola* and peanut butter crackers in little packages. Genna's aunts and cousins would almost always be there, too. Laughter, stories, and her grandfather's singing still resonate with Genna. Christmases were the best with presents piled against the walls, the smells of fresh coffee and pecan pie filling the air. "They were happy, happy times," Genna remembered. "So happy that we would leave for home, get over the long bridge, turn around, and go back to give them one more hug and kiss."

Closer to home, Virginia and Genna sometimes would take a picnic lunch, "magical words" for Virginia, and set out on a short road trip. Genna recalled one Saturday when she was about five years old that she and her mother drove to south Taylor County with its scenic mesas, the perfect setting for a picnic at a roadside park. "She and I sat on the ground stacking little houses and making fenced-in corrals from pebbles and fallen cedar bark," Genna recalled. "It remains a life-long memory for both of us." More recently, the two packed chicken salad sandwiches and drove to the same area. They listened to old music and relived the "good old days." Virginia even remembered a time she was in New York City and broke a little toe. She "never missed a beat," Genna said, as Genna's daughters, Bronwyn and Sundi, both nurses, were on the trip. They obtained supplies, taped the toes together and Virginia was on her way.

Virginia's impromptu medical treatment on herself and her determination not to let anything as insignificant as a broken toe get in her way were emblematic of the know-how and spunk that helped her succeed in the medical field. She was quick to give credit, too, and one of the people she gave much credit to was Earl M. Collier, administrator at Hendrick Memorial Hospital when Virginia opened her practice in 1940. "He was kind and he treated me well," Virginia recalled. Collier, born in 1898 in St. James, Missouri., taught school at age 17, then served in the U.S. Army during World War I. In 1926, he was named an administrator of Missouri Baptist Hospital in St. Louis.[3] Three years later, at age 31, Collier and his wife, Wilma, moved to Abilene when Collier was hired as administrator of West Texas Baptist Sanitarium.

Shortly thereafter, the stock market crash of 1929 hit with full force, and the hospital fell on hard times. As the Great Depression set in, the hospital was on shaky ground until Collier and the trustees got financial assistance from oilman T.G. Hendrick and his wife. In gratitude, the hospital trustees renamed the facility Hendrick Memorial Hospital in 1936.[4] Collier was well established and en route to making his own name in the medical administration field when Virginia arrived in 1940. Collier was a charter member and regent of the American College of Hospital Administrators. By 1965, five years before he retired, Collier was so highly respected that the Texas Hospital Association presented him with its inaugural Earl M. Collier Award for Distinguished Hospital Administration. The award has been presented annually since then. In naming the award for Collier, the Texas Hospital Association said of him: "Collier is considered the dean of hospital administration in Texas. He was respected for his philosophy of improving patient care, the driving force behind his administrative acts and decisions."[5]

That philosophy and Collier's legendary compassion were two traits that Virginia not only admired but lived by, too. Virginia recalled an incident with Collier in the 1940s when the hospital, like most American institutions of the time, was segregated. Virginia was on duty at the hospital when an Arab was brought in for treatment. He had boarded a bus in Houston not long after having a tonsillectomy, and the incision had started bleeding badly. Virginia recalled that African-Americans, other "dark-skinned people" and indigents were placed in quarters in the hospital's basement during those years. The man was indignant, and Collier had him moved to one of the best rooms in the hospital, Virginia recalled. The man was started on antibiotics, but the bleeding persisted. Unfortunately, Virginia said that even though people in the hospital were going out of their way to make the man comfortable, he wasn't pleased.

He continued to demand that someone make the bleeding stop, to which Virginia replied, "I'm doing everything I can to stop it besides putting my heel in there." Eventually, she did stop the bleeding and after a sufficient healing time, the man was put back on a bus to continue his journey. Virginia did not submit a bill for her services, but she later received a check from the government to cover expenses. She suspected that Collier submitted the bill for her. In addition to curing the ailing patient, Virginia made sure he had a good book to read on the continuation of his bus trip to California. Dale Carnegie had published a book in 1936 titled, *How to Win Friends and Influence People*. Virginia, thinking the book the perfect parting gift for the hard-to-please patient, purchased a copy, gave it to him, and sent him on his way.

Virginia's reputation as an excellent physician, compassionate Christian, and pragmatist grew over the years. A former family neighbor, Mary Anne Barker, who later moved to Abilene and then Dallas, recalled relying upon Virginia's skills and reputation when Barker's son was about ten years old. The youngster had flu-like symptoms and Barker took him to his pediatrician. The prescribed medicine had little effect, and her son continued to have a high temperature. Not knowing what else to do, Barker called Virginia at home on a Sunday afternoon. Without hesitation, Virginia instructed Barker to "meet me at the office in 15 minutes." She did as instructed and with the desired results. "He was well in three days," Barker recalled years later, still obviously impressed with Virginia's attitude and skills.

Two people who know well Virginia's reputation and have watched it only grow larger over the years are Boone Powell Jr. and his wife, Peggy Powell. Boone Powell succeeded Collier when Collier retired as Hendrick administrator on June 1, 1970. Collier stayed on at the hospital as director of development until retiring fully on December 31, 1975. Powell had worked as associate administrator at the hospital under Collier's leadership. The Powells and Virginia also were friends from their church, First Baptist. Powell learned

Virginia in front of her office on Hickory Street.

well under Collier's guidance. In 1980, at age 43, he became President and Chief Executive Officer of the Baylor Health Care System in Dallas, where he worked until April 2000, when he became chairman.[6] Now retired, Powell said that as he has grown older, "my admiration has gone way up" for pioneers like Virginia. Over the years, Powell has seen vast changes in the ratio of men to women in medical schools, which "wouldn't have happened without people like Virginia."

Powell remembered that Virginia was an active member of the medical staff when the two worked together at Hendrick, always interested in what was going on at the hospital and with her peers. Virginia fit in with the otherwise all-male staff and was highly respected as a physician and person, Powell recalled. "She was a sterling member of the medical profession," he said. "She gets five stars from me." Boone and Peggy Powell also were friends with Virginia from their involvement at First Baptist Church. As many others would attest, Virginia was just as enthusiastic and "all-in" at church as she was in her office, at home with Genna, or at the hospital. "She was not a talker, she was a doer," was the way Peggy Powell described her. She remembered Virginia being equally at home treating illnesses and "shampooing heads" in Abilene's poorer neighborhoods and on foreign mission fields. Less noticeable was Virginia's generosity in unlikely places like the dining room of the Abilene Country Club. Peggy Powell recalled that Virginia frequently filled a table for Sunday lunch with guests who couldn't pay her back. Perhaps they were new in town or people Virginia knew who never would have dined so well without her invitation. "She is a model of a gracious, compassionate Christian," Powell said. "She loved the word of God" and lived it.

One of Abilene's most noted obstetrician/gynecologists, the late Dr. R. Lee Rode, came to Abilene in 1950, ten years after Virginia. He recalled in an interview in March 2010, what a good physician Virginia was and how her patients loved her. "I thought it was great," Rode, who died January 17, 2011, said in the interview. At Rode's funeral service on January 20, 2011, Dr. Eduardo Rivera, senior pastor at St. Paul United Methodist Church, noted in his eulogy that the beloved physician delivered more than 11,000 babies during his years of practice in Abilene. Rode was held in high esteem in Abilene, and he recalled that he and most other male physicians admired and respected Virginia. "They may have treated her as more than an equal," he said. "They certainly didn't look down on her." Other peers had the same impressions. From 1961 to 1966, Dick Spalding was administrative assistant at Hendrick Memorial Hospital, which became Hendrick Medical Center in 1976. From August 1973 through February 1983 Spalding worked in various capacities with Hendrick, including interim president of the Medical Center and Founding President of Hendrick Medical Center Foundation. Spalding, who now is President of Serenity Foundation of Texas, recalled Virginia as being an "elegant, classy lady walking the halls of the hospital." A trait that Virginia still is known for was evident in those days as well. "She made it her business to know everybody," Spalding recalled. "She treated the cleaning person the same as the doctors." Spalding realized that Virginia's journey to her place "in a man's world" couldn't have been easy, but she would be the last to complain. "My observation," Spalding said, "would be that she probably fought for everything she got, but you wouldn't know it." Dr. Austin King is a current ear, nose, and throat specialist in Abilene who is well aware of Virginia's legacy. The fact that she was not only a physician at a time when few women chose that path, but also a specialist was remarkable, King noted, calling Virginia a "real trailblazer for women physicians."

Former patients have the same recollections as her peers of Virginia's professional attitude and her kindness. One of those is a man who went on to become quite famous in the world of academia—Dr. Bryce Jordan, who was president of Penn State University from 1983 until 1990, when he was named president emeritus. In 1996, Jordan's name was immortalized when the university named its newly constructed University Park arena The Bryce Jordan Center. Born in Clovis, N.M., and raised in Abilene, Jordan attended Hardin-Simmons University one year and then served in the U.S. Army Air Corps from 1942 to 1946. After earning both bachelor's and master's degrees in music from the University of Texas at Austin, Jordan taught at Hardin-Simmons from 1949 to 1951. He earned his doctorate in historical musicology with a minor in comparative literature from the University of North Carolina at Chapel Hill in 1956. Eventually, Jordan became chairman of the Department of Music at the University of Texas at Austin. From there, he was named vice president for student affairs at the university and then was named president ad interim of the campus. A year later, Jordan was named president of the University of Texas at Dallas. In 1981, Jordan was named Executive Vice Chancellor and Chief Operating Officer for Academic Affairs of the University of Texas System. That launched him to the presidency of Penn State University in 1983.[7]

Now retired and living in Austin, Jordan still has fond memories of Virginia. Jordan graduated from Abilene High School in 1941 and entered Hardin-Simmons at age 16. He left a year later to join the U.S. Army Air Corps and returned in 1949 to teach at Hardin-Simmons. During those years, Jordan's mother and Virginia were friends, and Virginia treated the family's eye, ear, nose, or throat needs. Jordan recalled that he had perfect 20/20 vision but that Virginia fitted him with eyeglasses to relieve eye strain. More importantly, he remembered her demeanor and professionalism. "I remember enjoying seeing her," Jordan said. "She was very kind." He also said neither he nor other family members thought anything about Virginia's being a "woman doctor." However, as the photo caption in the March 20, 1949, issue of the *Abilene Reporter-News* had noted, Virginia had a striking physical trait that made an impression on folks. "I remember she was a blonde," Jordan said. Since those early days, both Jordan and Virginia have been inducted into the Hardin-Simmons University Hall of Leaders, Jordan in 2003 and Virginia in 2004.

Virginia at Baptist World Alliance in Toronto 1979

BY LORETTA FULTON

Chapter 6
INFLUENCING OTHERS

*"She held her own because she was good and
confident and kind and caring."*
∞ Dr. Carl Trusler, Abilene physician who was treated
by Virginia as a child

By the end of her first decade in practice, Virginia was well-established among the medical fraternity in Abilene and was beginning to pave the way for others. The second female physician on record in Abilene was Dr. Melba McNeil. *The Archives of Pediatrics & Adolescent Medicine*, formerly the *American Journal of Diseases of Children*, lists a case report by McNeil in its May 1947 volume. The report is titled "Congenital Diaphragmatic Hernia on the Right Involving the Ascending Part of the Colon."[1] Little record other than that journal entry exists on McNeil. A more prominent female physician came on the scene in the early 1950s with the arrival of Dr. Mary Booth Steward, an anesthesiologist. A 1941 graduate of Abilene High School, Steward was the daughter of Greek immigrants Peter Dimitri Booth and Panayota Vletas Booth, whose friends called her "Mary." Of the couple's four children, three entered the field of medicine. After graduating from Abilene High, young Mary Booth attended McMurry College, Hardin-Simmons University, and the Hendrick Medical School of Nursing before enrolling in the Southwestern Medical College of the University of Texas from 1945 to 1949. She served an internship at Harris Memorial Hospital in Fort Worth and then a residency at Parkland Memorial Hospital in Dallas. In 1950, she married oilman James Willard Steward and the couple settled in Abilene in 1953.

In 1988, Steward was selected as an Abilene Pathfinder, the same year as Virginia. The write-up in the *Abilene Reporter-*

News noted that Steward was the first woman anesthesiologist in Taylor County and one of the first women doctors in Abilene. She also was the first anesthesiology resident at Parkland in Dallas before moving to Abilene. "At first, we were looked upon as unusual," she said. "Now we're pioneers."[2] During her career, Steward was chief of anesthesiology at Hendrick Memorial Hospital, renamed Hendrick Medical Center in 1976, and at St. Ann Hospital. She also was an anesthesiologist at Abilene State School, McKnight State Hospital in San Angelo, and at Dyess Air Force Base Hospital in Abilene.

After high school, Steward wondered what she would do with her life. She decided she wanted to be a doctor, but with two brothers already in medical school, she didn't think that would be possible. She spent one year in nursing school between her stays at McMurry and Hardin-Simmons but decided that wasn't for her. She wanted to be a doctor and one of the people who assisted her in that effort was Wilma Collier, wife of Earl M. Collier, the longtime administrator at Hendrick. Wilma Collier was one of Mary Booth's chemistry lab instructors at Hardin-Simmons and took the young lady under her wing. She wrote a letter of recommendation that helped Booth get into medical school. Steward still credits Collier and Virginia as being great boosts to her career. After settling in Abilene in 1953 with her husband, Steward found that Virginia already had paved the way. Male physicians were not resistant to the arrival of the lady anesthesiologist. "They had already accepted Virginia," Steward said.

The same year that Steward started practicing in Abilene–1953–Virginia's own life took another major turn. She married Abilene oilman Ed Connally, whose involvement with state and national politics, in addition to international business associations, would take the couple around the world and into social circles that seemed far removed from their quiet lifestyle in Abilene. But the day-to-day life in Abilene was what Virginia cherished most, to the extent of successfully discouraging Ed from running for Congress. Beginning in the 1950s, Virginia took on an additional role that kept her quite busy in Abilene. In addition to her private practice, hospital rounds, and involvement with the local medical society, Virginia became the physician for Hendrick Home for Children. The home, which today maintains its original campus in Abilene and a ranch in a neighboring county, was founded in 1939 by Thomas G. and Ida Nations Hendrick, the same couple who had saved the local hospital that today bears the Hendrick name. After the couple lost their only child, four-year-old Joseph, they established the home to serve children during the Great Depression.[3]

Children growing up at the home probably weren't impressed at all that they were being treated by Abilene's first female physician. But a couple of things about Virginia did stand out—her kind, gentle manner and her Rolls Royce Silver Cloud. Dr. Carl Trusler, an Abilene physician since 1979, was just "Carl" when he met Virginia for the first time. Carl, a sister and a brother, moved into Hendrick Home for Children in 1955. Their mother had been stricken with polio and their father was an alcoholic. Carl lived at Hendrick Home through 1964, when he graduated from Abilene Cooper High School. Thanks to the generosity of the home, he went to college at Hardin-Simmons University and earned a medical degree– all free of charge. After medical school and service in the Navy, Trusler returned to Abilene and opened a practice in family medicine in his hometown. He gives Virginia and Ed Connally, as well as Hendrick Home for Children, much of the credit for his inspiring success story. Trusler's recollection of his first encounter with Virginia has been echoed across Abilene hundreds of times over: "She prescribed my first pair of glasses." Trusler remembered Virginia coming to the home to tend to the children, as well as staff members taking the young patients to her office, then on Hickory Street. "Virginia was just always kind and a motherly sort to us," Trusler recalled. As young Carl grew older he began to take an interest in medicine. Virginia's cousin and Abilene physician, Dr. Joe Snow, would take Carl and a friend to the operating room with him, where Carl's interest in medicine grew even stronger. In retrospect, Trusler noted that Virginia "held her own in what is still a male-dominated world." She was always gentle and non-assertive, which Trusler believes was an asset with her male peers. "She held her own because she was good and confident and kind and caring," Trusler said.

Another trademark of Virginia in those days was the white Rolls Royce Silver Cloud she "tooled around town in," as Trusler recalled. Virginia admits a fondness for "nice cars," after purchasing a green Plymouth with her first earnings as a physician. Before the Rolls Royce, which Ed obtained in an oil deal, she drove a spiffy Ford Thunderbird. She loved the Rolls for its "high, solid ride that made you feel really good." The only thing Virginia didn't like about the car was the high price of maintenance that came with it. Once after a minor accident, Virginia recalled, paint had to be ordered from England. She only owned the car a few years, but it made quite an impression around town–especially with the youngsters at Hendrick Home for Children. The girls weren't as impressed as the teenage boys, who Virginia allowed to drive the luxury car. To the girls it was "that old-fashioned car" but to the boys it was a sight to behold. The girls may not have been impressed with the looks of the car, but they did love the little fold-down tables in the back that made the perfect setting for a picnic. One of Virginia's favorite treats was to make sandwiches, pick up the girls from the home, go to a park, fold down the tables and have a picnic.

The extravagant luxury car was easily recognizable around Abilene and could have given the wrong impression to anyone who didn't know Ed and Virginia Connally well. Virginia admittedly loved expensive clothing, accessories, and cars–she and Ed had matching Cadillacs in the 1960s. Hers was white and his was black. But that was just one trait the couple shared. A much larger part reflected the compassionate Christianity that both practiced. Indeed, Virginia found in Ed a companion and soul mate she didn't have in her first marriage. "That was just as happy as the other marriage had been unhappy," Virginia said. "Whatever he did, I enjoyed. He liked whatever I was interested in, too."Virginia recalled that on trips to Europe, Ed loved looking at pipes. He had quit smoking cigarettes and liked a good pipe. He also enjoyed shopping for leather goods and other "things men like," Virginia said. In turn, she enjoyed shopping for more delicate items like finely crafted figurines and silk goods. Neither seemed to tire of enjoying shopping for what the other liked. "I would look at things with him,"Virginia recalled."And he would look at things with me." As Virginia's daughter, Genna, put it, "Mother and Dad were a matched team. Each had the answers for the other." Genna fell in love with Ed early into the marriage. In 1950, Virginia had built a beautiful new home on Sayles Boulevard in Abilene, where she lives today. She and Ed chose the living room for their wedding site in 1953. Genna remembered that after the wedding, she left with her grandmother, an aunt and cousins for Galveston.

When the family reunited in Abilene, Genna recalled times were good. On Sundays, the three would eat a big breakfast at a popular cafeteria near First Baptist Church. After church, each would buy a container of ice cream and drive the countryside checking on Ed's wells, hurriedly eating their ice cream before it melted. Genna remembered Ed climbing up the metal steps on the side of an oil storage tank, opening the hatch, sniffing deeply and shouting, "Smells like money!" Genna loved her new dad's sense of humor and his compassion. She also liked the way he dressed–thanks to Virginia. She made sure he was clothed in a style she was accustomed to. Genna recalled Virginia and Ed going to Neiman-Marcus department store in Dallas to pick out his clothing. "Success was written all over him," Genna recalled. He returned the shopping favor by solving the dilemma of drapes for the living room and study of the spacious house on Sayles Boulevard. Ed volunteered to undertake the project, bringing a decorator from Dallas to assist. Problem solved. "It was done in a matter of a few months and was changed only once in 50 years," Genna said.

To this day, not much has changed at the stately home at

866 Sayles Boulevard, other than routine maintenance and occasional updates. But much has happened there since the 1950s, as an array of relatives, influential religious, political, and social leaders, friends and acquaintances have graced Virginia's home. A niece, Ann Ahearne, daughter of Virginia's sister Ruth has vivid memories of spending time with "Sissy" and her intriguing home. Growing up, Ahearne's family lived in Temple and would occasionally travel to Abilene for Christmas. Her aunt's home was a fun house to explore. Ahearne recalled one Christmas discovering a small chest of drawers. "I was positive that I heard jingle bells," Ahearne said, "which obviously could only mean reindeer on the roof." The closets and all the marvelous clothing they held also fascinated the young lady. They were filled with impeccable, tailored clothing and accessories. Ahearne remembered marveling at her aunt's ability to be a wife, mother, and doctor of medicine, "and be dressed to the nine's and wear heels doing it!" More importantly, Ahearne recalled the relationship her mother and aunt shared, plus the lessons she learned from her aunt "Sissy."

Ahearne remembered that her mother and aunt "had an incredible connection," borne out by the lengthy letters they shared and weekly telephone conversations at a time when making long distance phone calls was an expensive endeavor that not everyone could afford. Ahearne heard stories about her aunt from her mother and saw first-hand what a unique person Virginia was. She taught me, "if you want to do it, you can do it," Ahearne said. "That kind of determination, that kind of spirit is what can influence so many people." Ahearne counted herself fortunate to be "inside the bubble," which gave her a unique view how influential her aunt was. When Ahearne was in junior high school at an impressionable age, she started hearing from her mother and others about the wondrous things her aunt had done. Ahearne attended Hardin-Simmons University during the 1974-1975 school year before transferring to what is now the University of North Texas in Denton. "I was surprised everyone knew her," Ahearne said of her year at HSU.

Two grandsons from Ed's side of the family, Matt and Sid Roberts, also recalled the marvelous house in Abilene and their intriguing and influential "grandmother," Virginia. Sid credited his mother, Edwina Roberts, who was Ed's daughter, for allowing him and his siblings to have "three grandmothers." Ed's children were from a previous marriage. Sid, a radiation oncologist in Lufkin, Texas, recalled visits with Ed and Virginia were always special because of their lifestyle and circle of influence. "Visiting Virginia was always exotic," Sid recalled. "You never knew who would be next door in the mission house or at the church." Later in Sid's life, the names of Speaker of the U.S. House of Representatives Sam Rayburn and President Lyndon Johnson were as likely to be mentioned in the Connally home as the name of the person next door. "It was heady territory," Sid recalled.

A greater influence for both Matt and Sid than the "heady" stuff was the emphasis that Ed and Virginia placed on education and the manner in which Virginia practiced medicine. That influence extended to both men entering medical fields. Matt is a dentist in the East Texas city of Crockett and is past president of the Texas Dental Association. Sid was elected president of the Texas Radiological Society for 2011. Like so many others, Matt got his first pair of glasses via Virginia's skilled hands. He recalled hearing stories about Virginia "being a woman doctor" as he was growing up. Those stories obviously made an impression. "It was quite a significant factor," Matt said. "She was quite remarkable." Matt and Sid grew up in Midland, Texas, which is about 150 miles west of Abilene. Spending time with Ed and Virginia was a treat for both boys. Sid remembered that when he was about six years old, he spent a week with his grandfather and Virginia. The couple would take little Sid along on their 6 a.m. walks each day. "I was amazed they could walk as fast as they did," was Sid's primary recollection of those early visits. As the boys grew older, more important memories began to form. The Rolls Royce that Virginia drove signified more than wealth and luxury to impressionable young boys, Sid recalled.

"If ever there was a snapshot picture of the importance of education, there it was."

By the time Sid was in junior high school, he realized that he had to study hard, make good grades, and go to college to be successful in life. He also saw in the lives Ed and Virginia led that "success" meant more than driving luxurious cars and traveling in influential circles. "The money and influence was used to witness, to support ministry, to reach out on an international scale that I didn't see anyone else doing," Sid said of Ed and Virginia. He saw in Virginia that "medicine was a calling and a profession, not a job." When Sid graduated from Midland Lee High School in 1979, he enrolled in Houston's prestigious Rice University, intending to study music. A gifted pianist, Sid eventually drifted from that field and instead earned a medical degree from Baylor College of Medicine in 1987. Virginia's influence gets some of the credit for that decision. "I had a vision and a picture of what a physician should be, based on her," he said. "She took care of everybody–regardless." That practice sprang from Virginia's faithful adherence to Christian principles, another influence that stuck with the grandchildren. Sid recalled going with Virginia to a Baptist encampment in Glorieta, New Mexico, for Foreign Missions Week. There he met influential missionaries like Keith and Helen Jean Parks, longtime friends of Virginia and Ed. He saw Virginia's personal involvement in missions. She didn't just write a check. She took an active part in the lives of missionaries she supported and also donated her own time to short-term medical missions.

Virginia and Ed led busy, fulfilling lives, both separately and together. They shared many of the same interests and made every effort to be supportive when interests didn't match. Such was the case when Ed ventured into politics in the early 1950s. "I still had an office to run," Virginia said, and left the politics to her husband. But true to form, Virginia eventually got somewhat involved in Ed's world, although not to the same extent. "Anything I could do with Ed, I enjoyed," was Virginia's reason for being a trooper.

Ed Connally with Lyndon Johnson

Chapter 7

ED CONNALLY AND
THE WHIRLWIND YEARS

"He inspired me to do more and be more."
∞ Bill Petty, family friend, commenting on Ed Connally

On the day that Ed and Virginia were married, July 7, 1953, Dwight D. Eisenhower was president of the United States. By the time of Ed's death 22 years later in 1975, four more presidents would fill the office, and Ed and Virginia would be in the thick of things for much of it. The same year that the couple married, another event occurred in Ed's life that at the time didn't seem anywhere nearly as momentous as his marriage. But as history unfolded, it turned out to be the beginning of a remarkable ride for both Virginia and Ed. In October 1953, then-Senator Lyndon Baines Johnson was booked as a speaker at the Abilene Kiwanis Club. Six years later, when Connally was selected as head of the Texas Democratic Party, *Abilene Reporter-News* writer and Assistant Editor Katharyn Duff recalled that Connally had been selected to introduce Johnson at the 1953 Kiwanis luncheon primarily because of Connally's tendency to steer clear of political skirmishes.[1] Connally agreed, and when it came time to introduce the speaker, he said simply, "I present Senator Lyndon Johnson."

Duff recounted that from the beginning, Connally and Johnson developed a friendship and that, "the Abilenian credits the senator with some good political coaching, particularly in the fine art of getting things done while antagonizing as few as possible."[2] Duff also noted that early in his political career, Connally began a friendship with Price Daniel, a United States Senator from 1952 until 1956, when he resigned to run for governor of Texas. Daniel was governor from January 1957 to January 1963. In 1956, the year Daniel was elected governor, Connally "really began growing up politically," Duff reported in her 1959 account of Connally's selection to head the state Democratic Party.[3] In 1956, Connally was named to the State Democratic Executive Committee from the 24th Senatorial District. He also was elected chairman of the 17th Congressional District delegation to the 1956 Democratic National Convention in Chicago. In the summer of 1956, according to Duff's account, Connally staged a "harmony dinner" in Abilene with Byron Skelton, the new national committeeman, as guest speaker."[4]

But it was in the fall of 1956 that Connally really made his mark politically, according to Duff's article. Connally had spearheaded a fundraising "Democrat Day" on Tuesday, October 16, 1956. According to a write-up in that day's afternoon edition of the *Abilene Reporter-News,* "a flood of state and national Democratic Party leaders were pouring into Abilene" for the $100-a-plate dinner at the Windsor Hotel to be held that night.[5] According to the article, the dinner was expected to raise $20,000 for Democratic candidates. The dinner was so significant that attendees included Sen. Stuart Symington of Missouri, Speaker of the U.S. House of Representatives Sam Rayburn, then-Sen. Price Daniel, numerous other state and national Democratic leaders, and representatives of the Associated Press and United Press International.[6] The success of that 1956 dinner was credited with vaulting Connally to the top leadership position with the state Democratic Party in 1959. According to Katharyn Duff's article in the January 13, 1959, issue of the *Abilene Reporter-News,* few had expected the dinner to go over. "The Abilene area was strong for Eisenhower," Duff wrote, "and the country was in the middle of a drought that left many loyal Democrats short on cash."[7]

By the time Ed's reign as head of the state Democratic Party ended, few doubted his abilities. In December 1961, an overflow crowd at the Windsor Hotel ballroom paid tribute to Connally's service as party chairman. Telegrams from Washington and Austin were read, and numerous dignitaries

Ed and Virginia at Conn Music display at an Abilene Chamber of Commerce dinner in 1973.

were in the audience.[8] The first message read aloud was from President Kennedy, who lauded Connally's "many valuable contributions to the strength of the Democratic Party organization in Texas as well as to the national party."[9] Perhaps even more pleasing to the Connallys were remarks made by their pastor at First Baptist Church, Dr. Elwin L. Skiles, who described the "other side of Ed Connally, the side most persons don't know about."[10] Skiles noted that for several years the Connallys had paid the expenses of Helen Jean Parks as a Baptist missionary to Indonesia. Skiles also said Ed Connally had demonstrated his sincerity as a Christian when, on several occasions, he telephoned Skiles to say,

"Pastor, I want you to talk with someone about the church and becoming a Christian."[11]

A closer look at Ed Connally's life reveals how a remarkable blend of traits and experiences resulted in a man of Connally's abilities—a man able to pull off a national attention-grabbing event in Abilene, Texas, in 1956. Ed's grandson, Sid Roberts, recalled years later how impressed he had been with the emphasis that both Virginia, a medical school graduate, and Ed, with little formal schooling, placed on education. Sid remembered that on his visits to Abilene, Ed was constantly reading, trying to make up for a lack of formal education. An innate intelligence and curiosity served Connally well all his life, leading him to venture into the oil business with considerable success and into the thick of big-time politics, where he was one of the behind-the-scenes players who made things happen. As Virginia's daughter, Genna, who was nine years old when her mother married Ed, had noted, "success was written all over him."

James Edward Connally was born to Mr. and Mrs. J.R. Connally on May 22, 1909, at Markley, located in Young County in North Central Texas. The family consisted of the parents, six boys and two girls. Ed attended grade school in Dallas before the family relocated to Abilene, where Ed finished school in 1927. As a young man in Abilene, Ed worked in a grocery store and drove a truck. He later worked at a wholesale vegetable house. Later, he sold gasoline and tires and built a business that included a string of service stations before selling out and entering the oil business. He was so successful and astute that he eventually served in leadership positions with industry organizations such as the Independent Petroleum Association of America, the West Central Texas Oil & Gas Association, the Mid-Continent Oil & Gas Association, and the Texas Independent Producers and Royalty Owners Association. In a typewritten biographical sketch included in the *Abilene Reporter-News* morgue file on Connally, he described himself as "a man who is a little on the conservative side but liberal when it comes to dealing with human beings."

Nothing illustrates his "liberal dealings with human beings" as well as a story that Virginia still likes to tell. She recalled that a woman somehow managed to hoist Virginia's office safe onto a desk chair and wheel it out of the office. She later was caught and no doubt would have ended up in jail had Ed not intervened. When Ed found out the woman's personal circumstances—she was a single parent trying to raise a boy on little income—he decided that rather than press charges, he would pay the woman's way through beauty school so she could support herself and her son.

A keen business savvy, coupled with a sensitivity to human beings and their frailties, made Ed Connally a success in his chosen profession, politics, his personal life, and in the eyes of others. Not only was he highly thought of in state and national political circles, Ed also was admired by those who knew him best—his fellow Abilenians. He served on numerous local boards such as First State Bank, Central Airlines, Texas Law Enforcement Foundation, Missouri-Kansas-Texas Railroad Co. of Texas, Hardin-Simmons University, University of Texas School of Nursing Advisory Council, First Baptist Church, and the Abilene Chamber of Commerce. In 1958, he was named the first president of the newly formed Boys Club of Abilene, Inc., a forerunner to today's Boys and Girls Clubs of America.[12] A front page article in the *Abilene Reporter-News* announcing Connally's death in 1975 noted that he was one of eight civic leaders named in 1965 to consider the establishment of a two-year medical school in Abilene. And, in 1969 he headed a fund drive to garner scholarships for the Hendrick School of Nursing.[13]

Ed also influenced the lives of young people he encountered, whether through church activities or in the workplace. In the mid-1960s, Ed was looking for someone to add to the accounting department at his oil company. He consulted Dr. A. Overton Faubus in the business school at then-Abilene Christian College. Faubus, who died at age 96, on Aug. 1, 2010, is considered the patriarch of what is now the College of Business Administration at Abilene Christian

Ed Connally in 1972 photo from Abilene Reporter-News.

University. Faubus recommended Bill Petty, who had graduated in 1964 with a business degree, six months before Ed's request. Petty had roomed with a young man named Jack Griggs, who would marry Faubus's daughter, Ann, in 1963, so Faubus knew Petty well. Through that recommendation and Petty's subsequent employment at Connally Oil Company from 1964 to 1967, Griggs, Petty, and eventually their families, grew to love, admire, and appreciate both Ed and Virginia

Connally. "I just got to know and love them," Petty said. "I would see her coming back and forth to visit Ed."

Petty remembered Ed as being a mentor and an inspiration to him. He was perhaps a little stunned when Ed would let him listen in on conversations with Lyndon Johnson—with LBJ sitting in the Oval Office. But what impressed Petty even more than Ed's associations was the person Ed was. "He inspired me to do more and be more," Petty recalled. "You couldn't be around him without thinking, 'Who can I be? What can I do?'" Petty became so attached to Ed and Virginia that his friendship with Virginia continued after Ed's death. Over the years, Petty said he and his wife came to see Virginia as "one person making a difference—that's who she is. In our eyes, she's a spiritual giant." At the time of Ed's death in 1975, Petty was a professor of finance at Texas Tech University in Lubbock. Virginia called him and asked if he would run the business for her. "That was an honor for her to ask me," he said. But Petty was entrenched in the academic life and decided to stay on that course. Petty apparently made the right choice. He has been a professor of finance and holder of the W.W. Caruth Chair of Entrepreneurship at Baylor University in Waco since 1990. He was named the National Entrepreneurship Teacher of the Year in 2008 by the Acton Foundation for Entrepreneurial Excellence. In 2001, he received the Distinguished Professor Award from the Hankamer School of Business at Baylor.

Anyone who met Ed Connally would agree with Petty's assessment of his inspirational personal story and his personality. Ed seemed to those who knew him to be a man of boundless energy and interests. Once he delved into the world of politics, he put that energy and keen intellect to work. By the time he was through, he and Virginia would be hosting an annual birthday bash in Washington, D.C., for House Speaker Sam Rayburn. And, Ed would count former President Lyndon Johnson among his visitors to a Houston hospital when Ed had heart surgery in 1971. The Johnsons and others who walked on the largest political stages in the country would make their way to Abilene because of their association with Ed and Virginia Connally.

Virginia wasn't interested in politics to the extent that Ed was and even dissuaded him from a run at Congress. But she did enjoy certain aspects of the political life, including the social side. And in the 1950s and early 1960s, it didn't get much bigger socially than the annual birthday party for Speaker of the House Sam Rayburn of Bonham, Texas. A January 2, 1960, article in the *Abilene Reporter-News* reported that Ed and Virginia would be hosting the black-tie birthday dinner at the Mayflower Hotel in Washington, D.C., for the second year. The article noted that Rayburn's 79th birthday would fall on the following Wednesday, January 6, 1960, but that the dinner would be held on Thursday because of a scheduling conflict at the Mayflower Hotel. The Women's National Press Club dinner already was scheduled for January 6.[14] The article reported that approximately 80 guests, including all Texas members of Congress, had accepted the invitation from the Connallys "for their elegant party, which was one of the social high points of the year for the Texas group in Washington."[15] The article noted that among the guests would be some of Abilene's elite such as the commander of Dyess Air Force Base's 819th Air Division, Col. William Yancey and his wife, as well as *Reporter-News* publisher Howard McMahon and his wife.

The byline on the article read "By ELIZABETH CARPENTER Reporter-News Capital Bureau." By the time Liz Carpenter, as she was best known, died on March 20, 2010, she had made quite a name for herself in journalism, in Texas lore, and in political circles. Again, Virginia and Ed were in the mix of things. Born Mary Elizabeth Sutherland in Salado, Texas, on September 1, 1920, "Liz" was editor of her high school newspaper and studied journalism at the University of Texas at Austin. According to a *New York Times* news obituary, she was given a trip to Washington, D.C., as a college graduation present and decided to stay, finding a job as an assistant to the correspondent for 26 small Michigan newspapers.[16] According to the article, Carpenter also looked up her Congressman, Lyndon Baines Johnson, and found that he had gone off to war. Instead, she met his wife, Lady Bird Johnson, who was running the congressman's office. "It was the beginning of their long friendship."[17] In 1944, Liz married Les Carpenter, a high school sweetheart and fellow journalism student at the University of Texas. Among the wedding guests were the Johnsons.[18]

Liz Carpenter got a job with United Press International after the couple's wedding and they later organized the Carpenter News Bureau in Washington, reporting for about 20 newspapers in the Southwest. Les Carpenter died in 1974.[19] Liz went on to become LBJ's aide when he was vice president and worked as press secretary to Lady Bird Johnson during her White House years. She was in the motorcade in Dallas on November 22, 1963, when President John F. Kennedy was assassinated and Johnson ascended to the presidency. Liz wrote the brief speech Johnson delivered at the foot of Air Force One when he returned to Washington as the 36th President of the United States.[20] Out of the White House in 1971, Liz redirected her energy, fighting for women's causes, including the Equal Rights Amendment and the National Women's Political Caucus.[21]

In 1976, two years after the death of her husband, Liz returned to Texas, where she became a force in the Austin political and social scene. Perhaps as well known for her sometimes bawdy wit as her connections with the rich and powerful, Liz never failed to speak her mind, while remaining gracious at the same time. In 2003, she was guest speaker for a luncheon at the prim and proper Abilene Woman's Club. Among the guests, in addition to Virginia, were top administrators from Abilene's three private, church-affiliated universities. Liz managed to get in some slightly off-color humor without offending anyone. She was introduced by then-editor of the *Abilene Reporter-News*, Terri Burke, who called Liz a "Psalm-singing, foot-washing, born-again Democrat."[22] Living up to her reputation for both a quick wit and for being gracious, Liz paid a compliment to former President George H. W. Bush and his wife, Barbara. Liz told of receiving cards from the couple when Liz turned 80. Barbara Bush's birthday card said, "You aren't old–you were old last year." And the former president's note said, "It's time for a change–why not change parties?" The Bushes' good humor wasn't lost on Liz. "That's the way politics should be," she told the Woman's Club audience. "Pleasure, not poison."[23]

Virginia had met Liz in Washington when Lyndon Johnson was vice president under President Kennedy. "She was a rare person," as Virginia described her. Ed knew both Liz and Les Carpenter well and the two couples met often at political gatherings, including the 1960 Democratic National Convention in Los Angeles when the Kennedy/Johnson ticket prevailed. As Ed's and Virginia's grandson, Sid Roberts, had observed, being in their presence was often "heady."

Christmas card photo of Lady Bird Johnson and a great-grandbaby sits on Virginia's coffee table.

BY LORETTA FULTON

Chapter 8
HISTORIC MOMENT

"I would do anything I could for someone who loved my parents."
∞ Lynda Johnson Robb at
HSU Round Table Luncheon honoring Virginia

Sharing many of those heady years were two local women with their own stories to tell. Georgia Sanders is now retired after a long career first as a legal secretary and later as clerk of the U.S. District Court in Abilene. Another is Beverly Tarpley, retired attorney and wife of retired *Abilene Reporter-News* Editor Dick Tarpley. Sanders grew up in Arkansas and graduated in 1947 from then–Abilene Christian College with a degree in business administration. She returned to Arkansas after graduation, but on a return trip to Abilene for the wedding of her college roommate, Sanders learned of a job opening as a secretary to a local legend, Walter Raleigh Ely Sr. At the time, Ely had retired as judge of the 42nd District Court in Abilene and as chairman of the Texas Highway Commission. By the time he interviewed Sanders for a job, he was practicing oil and gas lease law and doing abstract and probate work. At the airport, Sanders' friend mentioned the job opening, with a warning: "The judge was particular and hard to please."[1] Undeterred, Sanders called "Judge Ely" and set up an interview, which apparently went extremely well. Sanders remained with Ely for 24 years, leaving only to move to the U.S. District Court in 1971. She remained there until her retirement in 1993.

Sanders recalled that she first met Virginia as a patient, while she was a student at Abilene Christian. She developed a sty on her eye and sought help from Virginia. "I went to her, and she took care of it," was Sanders' recollection of that first meeting. Later, when Sanders was entrenched in the legal world and as active as permissible in the political process while in the employ of the federal government, she got to know the Connallys on a different level. For years, Sanders has lived in a lovely home she designed just around the corner on an adjoining street to the Connally residence. About the same time that Sanders moved into her home, Ed Connally died. Sanders, Virginia, and some others from the neighborhood would set off at 6 a.m. daily for a one-mile walk. Through those daily visits, Sanders got to know Virginia well. "She was always so interesting and so smart and so pretty," Sanders recalled.

But long before that, Sanders found herself rubbing elbows with some of the biggest names in Texas and United States politics—at the same time as the Connallys. Sam Rayburn and Lyndon Johnson were frequent visitors to Judge Ely's office when Rayburn and Johnson held national political offices. When Sanders was still working in Ely's law office, one of her jobs had been to keep up correspondence on her boss's behalf with Congressmen and Senators. When they came to Abilene, she helped with registration at campaign fundraising events. To a young lady not long out of college, those were days to remember. "It was history," Sanders reflected. "Golly, I was fortunate."

Another woman enjoying those historic and "heady" days was local attorney Beverly Tarpley, who married *Abilene Reporter-News* courthouse reporter and later editor, Dick Tarpley in 1953, the same year that Ed and Virginia tied the knot. Through associates in the legal profession, Tarpley was introduced to Democratic Party politics and got to know the Connallys. Years later, when Tarpley was admitted to the United States Supreme Court, Lyndon Johnson was the Senate Majority Leader. A member of his staff introduced Tarpley to practice before the highest court in the land. Tarpley recalled that Ed was more involved in the political arena than Virginia. She and her husband, Dick, frequently bumped into Ed Connally at political functions, whether social or business. But not so much with Virginia. "She was a hard working doctor in those days," Tarpley recalled.

Even so, as Ed rose in political stature, Virginia's life became more intertwined with top political figures, none more notable than Lyndon and Lady Bird Johnson. Virginia, ever the quick study when it comes to sizing people up, pegged LBJ as a man who put his humble beginnings to good use. He knew the problems of the people around him, Virginia observed, and wanted to do something to improve their plight. "He knew how to use what he knew," is the way Virginia puts it. She also saw in Johnson a strong and knowledgeable man, and that was reassuring to her when he suddenly was thrust into the presidency. The top-level political connections came in handy for Virginia and Ed as they planned world travels for Ed's business and for the enriching experience. One such trip was planned for January 1964. In the fall of 1963, when LBJ was vice president, he assisted the Connallys in planning a trip to the Middle East. Johnson arranged for U.S. dignitaries stationed overseas to assist the Connallys in any way they could. Those connections, along with Ed and Virginia's personal contacts, made the trip a most memorable one. "We were met at airports by people representing our government and pharmaceutical representatives and missionaries," Virginia recalled. "We had the most interesting trip anybody could have."

Virginia and Ed were very much in the mix the day Johnson became president, just two months before the long-awaited trip. On November 22, 1963, Ed was returning to Texas from a business meeting in New York. He landed at Love Field in Dallas and spoke with some of the people who would be with President and Mrs. Kennedy and their entourage later that day. Ed then departed for Austin to attend the Texas Welcome Dinner, hosted by the State Democratic Executive Committee, honoring the Kennedys and Johnsons. Virginia would drive from Abilene to sit at the table that evening. She later learned that Ed was informed of President Kennedy's assassination while on the plane to Austin. Virginia found out after she arrived in Austin. "When we left, he was vice president," Virginia said of Johnson. "When we arrived, he was president." Virginia recalled that she and Ed just checked out of their hotel and headed home. "Everybody was in shock and was crying" was her dominant recollection of that tragic day.

Virginia was mentally whisked back to that eventful day on February 22, 2011, when the Johnson's older daughter, Lynda Johnson Robb, was guest speaker for the centennial luncheon of the Round Table organization at Hardin-Simmons University. The Simmons Round Table was founded in the fall of 1910 under the leadership of Lucile Sandefer, wife of university President Jefferson D. Sandefer, to cultivate friendships among faculty wives. Robb chose a question and answer format for her presentation, rather than a formal speech. One questioner asked her to share with the audience her memories of November 22, 1963, the day her father suddenly became president of the United States. Robb was a sophomore at the University of Texas and knew nothing of the assassination until a roommate called and told her to "stay right where you are, I'm coming to get you." Prior to that, she had been planning to attend the welcoming dinner that night in Austin for her parents and the Kennedys. The roommate came to take Lynda to a room that had a radio. In those days, Robb recalled, not many students had televisions in their room and only a few had radios. As Lynda and her roommate listened to news of President Kennedy and Governor John Connally being shot, and not yet knowing the outcome, they heard a loud voice announcing with authority, "Man on the floor!" In those days, Robb recalled with a laugh, men were not a common fixture in women's dormitories, as they are today. A dorm mother brought Lynda's Secret Service agent to the room and Lynda was escorted to the Governor's Mansion to await the news that would drastically change her life. At the conclusion of Lynda's talk at the Round Table luncheon, she walked to where Virginia was seated, gave her a big hug and spoke of the relationship Virginia had with her parents. Lynda said that when she was told Virginia would be at the luncheon, "I said I would do anything I could for someone

BY LORETTA FULTON

who loved my parents."

Ed and Virginia obviously didn't see the Johnsons as often following LBJ's ascension to the presidency, but after he left office, the couples renewed their friendship. Virginia recalled that Johnson and his entourage visited Ed in a Houston hospital when Ed had heart bypass surgery in 1971. A couple of years later, not long before LBJ's January 22, 1973, death from a heart attack, the former president and first lady invited the Connallys to their Central Texas ranch. Knowing he wasn't in good health, Johnson asked Virginia, "Why don't they do for me what they did for Ed in the hospital?" Virginia didn't hesitate with her reply, even if the man asking the question happened to be a former president: "I don't know," she said. "Why don't you ask them?" After Johnson's death, Virginia remained in close contact with Lady Bird and admires the late first lady's accomplishments to this day.

Among the many artifacts from world travels, personal mementos, and family photos that grace Virginia's living room is a framed Christmas card from Lady Bird, featuring a photo of the elated former first lady holding one of her great-grandchildren. When Lady Bird died July 11, 2007, a writer from the *Abilene Reporter-News* contacted Virginia for a reflective piece on the former first lady. Virginia told him the photo served as reminder of Lady Bird's "graciousness and nobility."[2] The article noted that Lady Bird was a frequent visitor to Abilene, speaking from time to time at the Abilene Woman's Club before her husband became vice president. Lady Bird, like many other well known personalities, also visited the Connally home. "We had tea here, and she sat at that little table right over there," Virginia told *the Reporter-News* writer, pointing to a small table in the living room. Virginia noted that Lady Bird never failed to thank people who attended fundraisers or other political functions. "She'd say, 'Virginia, give me a list of who was invited and who came.' And as soon as she'd get on the plane, she'd write them."[3]

An up close and personal encounter with the Johnsons in 1960 gave Virginia insight into the couple's relationship and how important Lady Bird was to her husband's success. As chairman of the Texas Democratic Party in 1960, Ed was a major player at the party's national convention held that year in Los Angeles. Virginia recalled the excitement of the convention, when John F. Kennedy was nominated for president, but not without a challenge from Johnson, who was Senate Majority Leader at the time, and from Adlai Stevenson II, the party's nominee in 1952 and 1956. Virginia recalled how busy Ed was, conferring with Johnson and Speaker of the House Sam Rayburn. One evening, Johnson was invited to speak at a gathering across town from the convention site and Ed and Virginia were invited to ride with the Johnsons to the venue in a limo. Ever observant, Virginia noticed how Lady Bird would talk to her husband about the speech, even giving advice on what to say and not to say. "It was real interesting to be in the car and see the interaction," Virginia said. "He would listen to her."

Over the years, the Connally and Johnson families became close enough that the two Johnson daughters were among the people sending congratulatory notes to the Abilene Woman's Club Legacy Award Luncheon in April 2009, when Virginia was named the inaugural recipient. Luci Baines Johnson wrote:

Dear Mrs. Connally:

Oh how I wish I could be with you to celebrate the presentation of the Heritage Legacy Award. I am so grateful that this honor is being bestowed upon you, as I am for the day that you came into our family's life.

Alas I have a direct conflict and am in London on a business (trip) with my husband Ian. I want to be with two loved ones who are miles apart in geography but very close in spirit.

Your service to the needs of the community has been a gift to the world. I am so happy for all of those who will be able to be in your presence today to celebrate you!

Please know that I am applauding the loudest from afar.

With a lifetime of love,
Luci Baines Johnson

Lynda Johnson Robb wrote:

I am delighted that you are honoring Dr. Virginia Connally. What dedication and perseverance she has had throughout her life. To receive a medical degree when most women didn't have even a college education is admirable. To be the first woman doctor in Abilene, what a pioneer.

There must have been such a great deal of pressure to be the perfect role model.

But, she found time to encourage and support a rising politician. My father and mother valued the support that she and her husband gave to them, to their community and to the Democratic Party. She did not sit on the sidelines and let others work for a better world. She jumped right in and gave her all.

Sincerely,
Lynda Johnson Robb

Virginia's reach into the political realm continued long after the Johnsons had left office, as evidenced by another congratulatory letter read at the April 2009 Woman's Club luncheon in which Virginia received the Legacy Award. This one was from New Mexico Governor Bill Richardson, who wrote in part:

As Governor of New Mexico, I am honored to send a special greeting as you gather with many of your friends. I would have loved to be with you today, to share memories of the past and to hear all of the new and exciting "tasks" as we call them, that you have planned for the future. If I can have your energy at the age of 97, I will know that God has blessed me with good health.

As Abilene's first woman physician and 42 years of practice, I cannot even touch the surface or give honorable mention to all whose lives you have touched. Humility, keen intellect, love of learning, and unwavering faith and service are qualities that you possess and are respected for.

With warmest regards,
Bill Richardson
Governor of New Mexico

Because of Virginia and Ed's close ties with the Johnson family and Ed's service as chairman of the state Democratic

Party, politics always will be a part of Virginia's life. In August 2010, a relative e-mailed Virginia a link to an interesting bit of history that he had found on the Internet. That history mentioned both John F. Kennedy and Ed Connally. The link was to a Web site for "Live Auctioneers." The featured item was a copy of Kennedy's inaugural address and carried the heading:

John F. Kennedy's January 20, 1961, Inaugural Address; A broadside copy printed in gold italic type on parchment paper with a gilt decorative border printed "Compliments of J. Ed. Connally, Chairman Democratic Party of Texas" lower center, in original mailing envelope with return address of Texas State Democratic Executive Committee, Abilene, Texas, with original paper clip securing broadside to cardboard backing, 11 ½" x 15 ½", VG+. Property of M.B. Gallagher.[4]

Starting bid was $50—not much, considering all the history contained on that decorative paper.

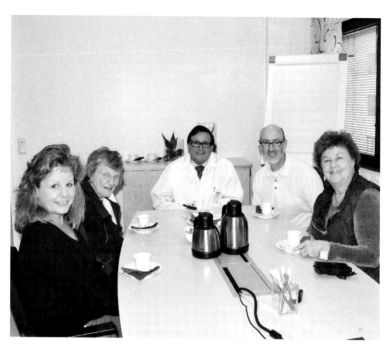

In September 2010 Virginia made her eighth trip to Finland with family members. While there, they visited a clinic owned by Dr. Sakari Alhopuro, center, in white coat. Virginia met Sakari, his parents, and brothers on a trip to Finland in the 1960s. From left are granddaughter Sundi Spivey, Virginia, Sakari, grandson Sid Roberts and daughter Genna Davis.

Chapter 9
GLOBE TROTTING

"Because I said yes a lot."

⌐ Virginia Connally on a lifetime of learning and adventure

In his biography of Danish philosopher and theologian Soren Kierkegaard, author Joakim Garff noted a trait that Kierkegaard shared with Socrates–one that might equally be applied to Virginia. Garff wrote that in Kierkegaard's *The Concept of Irony*, he called Socrates "a virtuoso of the casual encounter" on the streets and alleys of Athens, where he always "spoke with equal facility to hide tanners, tailors, Sophists, statesmen, and poets, with young and old, spoke with them equally well about everything."[1] That tendency has been a hallmark of Virginia's life, as well, and has led to casual encounters that developed into lifetime friendships and amazing experiences. As Virginia puts it, that outcome was, "Because I said yes a lot."

Virginia's opportunity to make casual encounters the world over came with her marriage to Ed in 1953. That union not only put her on the largest political stage in the country, it also opened opportunities for national and international travel that she had not experienced before. Virginia jokes about her bus trip to New Orleans shortly after she graduated from Simmons University in 1933 and married Fred Boyd in September of that year. That unpleasant trip on a hot bus with no air conditioning was her first outside her native Texas. Before that, her longest trip had been the one from her home in Temple to attend college in Abilene, a distance of about 180 miles. But all that changed when Dr. Virginia Boyd became Dr. Virginia Boyd Connally. Ed was a partner in Central Airlines, a feeder airline out of Abilene, and that partnership allowed the couple to travel free anywhere in the world. They made the most of it. Ed's oil business required numerous far-flung trips, and the couple enjoyed leisure travel, as well. Both soaked up the local culture and stored away memories for a lifetime.

Virginia's home is filled with artifacts from all corners of the world. When Ed and Virginia both moved into new offices in the same building they had constructed at 744 Hickory Street in 1962, the *Abilene Reporter-News* ran a lengthy article announcing an open house and describing the unique building. "The structure, of salmon colored brick, concrete and steel, was built in connection with a large, super-strong bomb and fallout shelter at an approximate cost of $100,000," the story stated.[2] Ed's office, in stark contrast to the sterile bomb shelter and Virginia's medical facilities, was decorated with fine furnishings from various parts of the globe. The *Reporter-News* article described an imported fireplace, silk wall covering from France, a rug from Peru, three rugs from Afghanistan, a marble top table and mantelpiece from Uruguay, tapestries from France, a painting from Italy and other items, including murals from all over the world.[3] Virginia's home is filled with beautiful, and unusual, mementos of global travel and the people encountered on those trips.

Typical of Virginia's casual encounters–and the long-lasting effects–was a chance meeting on a street corner in Helsinki in the 1960s. Some years later, Virginia wrote an account of the trip and titled it, "A Love Affair With Finland." In the first paragraph, she wrote, "This is a story of agape love. This story has no ending." Indeed, decades after that trip, the story continues. The trip truly turned into a lifelong love affair, with Virginia, grandson Sid Roberts, daughter Genna, and granddaughter Sundi returning in September 2010 for Virginia's eighth trip to Finland, the first Scandinavian country she ever visited. But as with all of Virginia's world travels, that first trip to Finland was much more than a sight-seeing excursion. She and Ed had one of those remarkable casual encounters that perceptive, inquisitive, and loving people turn into magical moments.

Virginia recalled that she and Ed walked out of their hotel

knowing absolutely no one in Finland and not speaking or understanding a word of the language. "As we stood on the curb looking at an area where people were crowded around booths with flowers and fruit and vegetables, Ed remarked, 'I wonder what that is,'" Virginia wrote in her "love letter" to Finland. Call what ensued fate, providence, or just plain luck. Whatever the encounter was, it sparked a lifelong friendship of mutual admiration. "This beautiful blonde young lady turned and asked us in perfect English with a charming Finnish lilt, 'This is our market place. Would you like me to show it to you?'" Typical of Virginia, she quickly said "yes." The brief introduction and tour of the marketplace was followed by dinner at the home of the beautiful woman, Ulla Maija Alhopuro, and her family. True to all of Virginia's encounters, this one had some interesting "coincidences." It turned out that Abilene's first female physician had just met Finland's "Outstanding Pharmacologist of the Year" in Ulla Maija Alhopuro. And her husband, Matti, was a well-known engineer in Finland, with interests similar to Ed's. The couple were the parents of three sons, including two who lived a year in the United States as participants in Youth for Understanding, a non-profit international educational organization founded in 1951. The program is still going strong, with 64 countries participating in 2010. At the time of the trip, Ulla Maija was a representative from Finland, and Virginia and Ed were friends with a representative of the organization who lived in Abilene–just another "coincidence" that seems to be a theme in Virginia's life.

That initial encounter spawned lasting friendships between Sid and the Alhopuro boys–Jorma, Sakari, and Markku–and now their children and grandchildren. "The friendship which began on a street corner in Helsinki flourished and became truly a love affair with a nation and its people," Virginia wrote. "For us, Finland became the Alhopuros. The Alhopuros were Finland." Ed and Virginia later returned to Finland as guests of the Alhopuros. In 1971, the Alhopuros carried on with a planned trip to the United States despite Ed having to enter

Methodist Hospital in Houston for heart surgery. "Friends and relatives responded to the emergency by taking this couple into their homes and entertaining and showing them our country and part of Mexico," Virginia wrote. Despite the deaths of Ed in 1975, Matti in 1994, and Ulla Maija in 1995, the extended families have remained in close contact, culminating with the return trip to Finland in September 2010. A poignant conclusion to Virginia's "A Love Affair With Finland," tells much about her spirit, her beliefs, and her outlook on life: "Now Ed and Matti and Ulla Maija are in a place where there is a universal language of love and understanding. They are retelling stories of bravery, conquest, quirks of different cultures on earth, probably wondering when God will have completed his work with me and will allow me to eat and sing and pray and even dance with them."

Following the family trip to Finland in September 2010, Virginia' grandson, Sid Roberts, published a book of photos and commentary. Virginia's remarks reflect the love of Finland, its history, traditions, and its people that first began to form in that first encounter. "If I couldn't live in Texas," she wrote, "I would want to live in Finland where there is peace and freedom, an appreciation of nature and families and nation." Sakari Alhopuro wrote admiringly of Virginia in his page in the photo album. He recalled Ed and Virginia's visits as he was growing up and the family's trips to the United States. Once, Sakari recalled, he was invited to give a lecture at the Mayo Clinic in Rochester, Minnesota, and visited Abilene while in the United States. "I learned of their generosity in the community and at the university, and I had many good discussions with Virginia about values in life." He, like anyone who knows Virginia, marveled at her spry, active lifestyle during the September 2010 trip as Virginia was approaching 98. "Virginia could not have done better," he wrote. "She was all the time happy and active and she wanted to see the old places and all new things as well." As for Virginia, she got a chuckle out of the younger folks' problems with jet lag after a long trip. "They kept fussing about waking up in the middle

Virginia and family saw many historic sites on a trip to Finland in September 2010. Among them were the Helsinki Cathedral in the background. From left are grandson Sid Roberts, daughter Genna Davis, Virginia, and granddaughter Sundi Spivey.

of the night. Well, I do anyway!" she said, noting that many days she awakens at 4 a.m. Not one to waste time tossing and turning, Virginia instead spends that quiet time writing and thinking.

Typical of Virginia, she still has a keepsake from one of her early trips to Finland–a partially squeezed tube of hand cream that she still uses sparingly. The encounter with Finland's "Outstanding Pharmacologist of the Year" came by accident, but Virginia and Ed's meetings with other people of note in foreign lands were by design. Connections in medicine, pharmaceuticals, business, and politics gave the couple entree to places most travelers wouldn't see. In

January 1964, barely two months after Lyndon Johnson was thrust into the presidency, Virginia and Ed toured Japan, Taiwan, Hong Kong, Taiwan, Thailand, Singapore, and India. They were guests of Ambassador to India and Mrs. Chester Bowles and enjoyed India's Republic Day parade on January 26, 1964. That Republic Day celebration turned out to be the last for Jawaharlal Nehru, the first prime minister of independent India, who died in May that year. After the Connallys returned to the United States, they hosted various Indian officials and business leaders in their Abilene home. While in Bombay (Mumbai since 1996) they were dinner guests, along with six other people, of Madame Vijaya Lakshmi Pandit, a sister to Nehru who in 1953 became the first woman elected president of the United Nations General Assembly.[4] A biography of Pandit from the *Encyclopaedia Britannica* described her as "one of the world's leading women in public life in the 20th century."[5] Pandit served as governor of the state of Maharashtra (Bombay) from 1962 to 1964. And from 1964 to 1968, she was a member of the Indian Lok Sabha, or parliament, representing the constituency formerly represented by her brother.[6] Ever observant, Virginia noticed something odd about the dessert served at the conclusion of the dinner hosted by Madame Pandit—it was sprinkled with silver flecks, apparently purely to enhance the presentation. On the way back to their hotel, Ed and Virginia mentioned the silver sprinkles to the driver, and he stopped at a shop so that Virginia could buy a stack of thin silver sheets separated by equally thin sheets of paper—another long-ago keepsake that Virginia still has in a drawer and is always thrilled to show visitors.

Virginia, of course, didn't let an opportunity go by to show God's love through an act of kindness and generosity on that trip. She recalled meeting a young boy shining shoes on Janpath Road in New Delhi. She learned later that Madame Pandit had been instrumental in an effort to teach young boys to shine shoes for money, rather than begging on the streets. But when Virginia encountered little A.B. Bhalla, she didn't know that. She also didn't need her shoes shined–nor did Ed–but Virginia's heart was touched. Putting both her pragmatism and her compassion to work, she struck up a limited conversation with the boy and decided on the spot that she wanted to help him have a successful future. Due to local laws concerning local currency, she arranged some time later to send the boy money. She still has a copy of a handwritten letter that A.B. sent her in August 1969, when he was a young teenager. Virginia had made good on her word, of course, and arranged to send money to Tehran, Iran, for A.B. to pick up. His letter said, "You will be glad to know that I am sailing tomorrow from Bombay. I will reach Basra on 24th. By 25th or 26th I will be in Tehran. There I will meet American consulate to collect the money. I think you must have sent my particulars to him. I will keep you informed about me wherever I am. I hope you will guide me and encourage me to success. I am indebted to you for your financial help, and the encouragement you gave me. With your good wishes and blessings, I hope I will be successful…Please write to me in Iran. Thanks. Loving Son, A.B. Bhalla."

Virginia's travels with Ed whetted her appetite for seeing the world and meeting its people. After Ed's death in 1975, Virginia set out on trips alone, or with a friend or group. Some of those–just like the first trip to Finland–led to introductions that Virginia still talks about. "Every trip I've had has been something special," she said. On one venture in 1982, Virginia and her travel companions had tea with Malcolm Muggeridge, the British author, journalist, and satirist who came to Christianity late in life after having been a professed agnostic for most of his life. Muggeridge, who died in 1990, published *Jesus Rediscovered* in 1969, a collection of essays, articles and sermons on faith. His personal story of conversion, coupled with his intellectual prowess, made him an ideal person for Virginia to share a cup of tea with. Virginia joined the tour after one member of the group, Bob Beckham, was unable to make it. Beckham's mother, Agnes Beckham, and Virginia were friends, so she asked Virginia to join the tour. Beckham's wife, Peggy Beckham, also made the trip and still has vivid memories of it. Host for the tour was Dr. Elton Trueblood, an author, educator, philosopher, and theologian, who in 1936 became chaplain at Stanford University. In 1945, he left Stanford to go to Earlham College in Richmond, Indiana, where he was a professor of philosophy until his retirement in 1966.[7]

A Quaker by faith, Trueblood was favored by people with a keen intellect who were deeply grounded in Christianity, no matter the denomination. Bob and Peggy Beckham are both Episcopalians, while Agnes Beckham, Bob's mother, was a member of First Baptist Church, along with Virginia. People who signed up for the trip to England with Trueblood were thinkers attracted to Trueblood's intellect and deep spirituality. Waynet.org, a Web site that chronicles the people and happenings in Wayne County, Indiana, where Earlham College is located, reprinted a brief biography of Trueblood that first was published in 1995 in the *Earlhamite*. The article stated that, "Avoiding simplistic admonitions for a 'back to church' or 'back to the Bible' movement, he called for the reinvigoration of religious faith as the essential force necessary to sustain the ethical, moral, and social principles on which a humane and livable world order could be built. He warned against what he called 'churchianity' and 'vague religiosity,' but he also cautioned against the overly optimistic expectations of secular social-reformism."[8]

His extensive writings and his personal theology appealed to Virginia and others on the trip. A highlight was the one-hour visit with Muggeridge, who was friends with Trueblood. "It was a real life-altering experience," Peggy Beckham recalled. The 40 or so people on the tour crowded into Muggeridge's library, sitting on every available chair and sofa—and even the floor—entranced by the discussion between Trueblood and Muggeridge. "You could just hear their great minds going back and forth," Beckham said. It was on that trip that Virginia also met Muggeridge's wife, Kitty, who translated *The Sacrament of the Present Moment* by Jean-Pierre De Caussade. The book is a favorite of Virginia's, and she often gives copies as presents. At the time of the trip, Muggeridge had not made his way back to the church. Trueblood admonished him to "work within the system and not be too critical," Beckham said. After the stimulating discussion, tea and cookies, the travelers boarded the bus to continue their journey. But before the bus started to roll again, Trueblood stood at the front and addressed the group. He asked them to pray that Muggeridge would find his way back to the church, Beckham recalled. The tour members later learned that two months after their visit, Muggeridge had converted to Catholicism because of his admiration for Mother Teresa, Beckham said. No one knows whether the prayers uttered on the tour bus came into play or if that was just a "coincidence."

Virginia in 1983 photo from Abilene Reporter-News taken at meeting of the National Board of the Medical College of Pennsylvania, established in 1850 as the Female Medical College of Pennsylvania, the first in the world for women physicians. From left are Dorothy Perkins of Eastland, Virginia, the late Washington journalist Sarah McClendon and an un-identified woman.

BY LORETTA FULTON

Chapter 10
MAKING FRIENDS NEAR AND FAR

"I didn't know anybody on the trip."
∞ Virginia Connally, on journeying to Russia in 1976

Although Virginia met many well-connected people in high places during her travels, she also developed relationships–even friendships–with ordinary people she happened to meet. She also developed a friendship with Janet Erwin, a former member of First Baptist Church, who would accompany Virginia on many of her journeys, assisting and sharing in new experiences. "She has been so good to go with me and be interested in the things I am," Virginia said. Erwin recalled that she was in charge of ladies missions when Virginia first invited her to be a travel companion. "We had fun," Erwin said. "It was kind of a natural thing." Over the years, Erwin has accompanied Virginia to church functions in various states and even traveled with her to England for a Baptist World Congress. The relationship has proven to be mutually beneficial, both ladies agree. "We found out we had some common interests," Erwin said. "I learned from her and she learned from me."

A lasting friendship and an opportunity to serve in a noteworthy position came about as the result of meeting a woman on a trip to Greece. The travel party consisted of eight women from various places, seven of whom were Methodists, and Virginia as the lone Baptist. All eight blended well, and Virginia developed a lasting friendship with one in particular, Dorothy Perkins of Eastland, which is about 55 miles east of Abilene. "We hit it off immediately," Virginia recalled. "We were Texans." The meeting turned out to be another of Virginia's remarkable casual encounters. Dorothy's mother, Emily Gleason Perkins, had served on the National Board of the Medical College of Pennsylvania, which was chartered in Philadelphia in 1850 as the Female Medical College of Pennsylvania, the first women's medical college in the world. In 1867, the school was renamed the Woman's Medical College of Pennsylvania, and in 1970 the name was changed to Medical College of Pennsylvania when the school began accepting male students. Since 2002, the school has been under the auspices of Drexel University in Philadelphia and is known as the Drexel University College of Medicine.[1] Dorothy told Virginia of her mother's active role in health issues and how she and other board members were selected, "because they were outstanding ladies in their world." In fact, some of the ladies carried impressive last names such as DuPont and Mars, as in candy bars. The ladies were involved in a wide range of endeavors, from music to politics to medicine. Virginia was thrilled to join such an august body. The January 10, 1983, edition of the *Abilene Reporter-News* carried a photo courtesy of the public relations department of the Medical College of Pennsylvania. A short item accompanying the photo noted that Virginia recently had attended the annual meeting of the college's National Board in Washington, D.C. The article stated that Virginia was "one of the 170 prominent members who serve as ambassadors of good will to promote nationally the interests and objectives of MCP."[2] Pictured were Virginia and Sarah McClendon, a pioneering journalist who died in 2003 at age 92. McClendon, a native of Tyler, was a longtime Washington correspondent noted for her sometimes aggressive questioning of presidents during White House news conferences.

During Virginia's tenure, the National Board met twice a year, in Philadelphia in the spring and in Washington in the fall. At other times during the year, Dorothy and Virginia would travel together. Dorothy's own voyage to Eastland, Texas, is interesting in itself. Her mother and father married in 1917 near Boston. Her father was a geologist and the family later moved to Oklahoma City where he was involved in the oil business. But Dorothy's grandmother on her father's side had been a "horse and buggy doctor" in her day, and

Virginia reads and relaxes in her home in this 1979 photo from the Abilene Reporter-News.

Dorothy's father thought she should follow in her footsteps. But Dorothy had different ideas. "I majored in English, and I'm glad I did," she said. The oil business eventually took the family to Eastland, and Dorothy stills lives in the family home. Before retiring to Eastland, Dorothy taught high school English in the 1950s and 1960s in Midland, which is about 150 miles west of Abilene. While Virginia was serving on the medical school board, the two ladies often traveled together. "I don't know how many embassies we went to," Virginia said. They also took in plays in New York City, and one memorable venture onto Broadway brought out another of Virginia's traits. She recalled going to see *Sweeney Todd, the Demon Barber of Fleet Street*, a 1979 musical based on the 1973 play by Christopher Bond. The cannibalistic "demon barber" part of the story was too much for Virginia, and she walked out of the theater, despite the high price of Broadway tickets. To her, the money was less important than wasting precious time on something that wasn't meaningful, or at least entertaining. "They can have my money, but they can't have my time" was her thinking then—and now. "There is so little

*Virginia's sister, "Babe" Ruth Williams, left, and cousin
Mercedes Callaway, center, with Virginia.*

time. I want to be sure to spend it well."

Dorothy and Virginia also had a memorable trip to
Massachusetts to stay in a house that Dorothy's great-great-
grandfather had purchased from the original owner. The
three-story Victorian house was built in 1837. Dorothy's
great-great-grandfather on her mother's side was the head
of a woolen mill in the region that made clothes for Union
soldiers during the Civil War. The house had remained in the
family since that original purchase. Dorothy made the journey
every summer to open the house after a long winter. One
year Virginia accompanied her and set about helping with
the myriad tasks necessary to re-open an aging house that
had been shut for months. Dorothy and Virginia both recalled
their ill-fated attempt to turn on the water. The aging pipes
and valves didn't want to cooperate but eventually gave way,

with disastrous results. "We had Niagara Falls in the house," Dorothy said, still getting a laugh out of the memory.

Virginia became a sought-after travel companion in a variety of circles. She was knowledgeable, full of pep, of good humor, and always filled with ideas. Bill Petty, who had met Virginia in 1964 when Ed had hired him to work in the accounting department at Connally Oil Company, recalled a family vacation to Europe in the early 1980s that included Virginia. The travel party consisted of Petty, his wife, Donna, their two daughters, a niece and nephew, Virginia and her granddaughter Sundi. Petty laughed remembering Virginia showing up with yellow bandanas for everyone to wear in case they got separated. She also made the trip even more fun by suggesting the group hand out "awards" at the end such as "most congenial" and "who was the most helpful." Like most people who have traveled with Virginia, the Petty family learned that keeping up with her can be a challenge. As the group traveled the countryside in a van, Virginia rode in the second row, always pointing to landmarks. "Look at this, look at that," Petty recalled her saying. "We couldn't keep up with her. She was just a leader on the trip."

Other travels took Virginia to such exotic and intriguing places as China and Russia. Virginia's spunk was on full display during the trip to Russia in 1976, following Ed's death in 1975. Virginia joined a group of doctors and aviators for the journey. "I didn't know anybody on the trip," she said, which would have discouraged most people from signing up. But not Virginia. Two days before the group was to depart from New York, Virginia traveled to the city by herself. She went in search of Bibles printed in English and Russian and finally found what she was looking for at the American Bible Society. "They had three Bibles, and I bought all three," she recalled. Once the group arrived in Russia, Virginia thought nothing of taking off on her own. When she couldn't get anyone to join her in attending a church service, she just caught a cab and went alone. She found a church, possibly Baptist, although she doesn't remember for sure. She does remember, though, that the church was surrounded by an extremely tall fence. The ominous sight might have signaled danger to some, but not Virginia. Perhaps bolstered by her strong belief that God sent her there for a purpose and her desire to deliver the Bibles, she calmly walked inside the fence and into the church. "I felt no fear," she said.

Virginia's deep religious convictions and her lifetime interest in missions led to her interest in an equally exotic country, China. Her strong interest in the country and its people came partly from her familiarity with Bertha Smith, a missionary to China, who lived to be 99. Smith was appointed a missionary by the Southern Baptist Convention Foreign Mission Board on July 3, 1917, and arrived in China on September 4 of that year. In 1965, she wrote a book titled, *Go Home and Tell*, which influenced Virginia to the point that she was determined to bring Smith to Abilene. As usual, she succeeded, enlisting Ed's aid. Virginia recalled that one year when Ed asked her what she wanted for her birthday, she replied that she wanted him to bring Smith to Abilene. "He got her here," Virginia said, although it was a year later. Virginia recalled that Smith stayed in a local hotel during her trip to Abilene. Known for her prayer discipline, Smith didn't disappoint her Abilene hosts. Virginia remembered that when she and a friend, Cleone Thornton, went to the hotel to pick up Smith, "She had us on our knees praying almost before we got in the door."

Virginia had gotten a taste of the Orient during a 1964 tour. In 1979, four years after Ed's death, she joined a tour group of 22 people for a 17-day return trip. As usual, the trip involved much more than sight-seeing. It was unusual from the beginning. A New York couple who had been investors in Connally Oil Company knew that Ed and Virginia wanted someday to return to Taiwan after their initial visit in 1964. They sent Virginia a book titled *The Fifth Chinese Daughter*, published in 1950 by Jade Snow Wong, a fine arts ceramicist who also owned a gift shop and travel agency in San Francisco with her husband, Woodrow Ong. Ed and Virginia had ties

*Virginia and friends celebrate a birthday. From left are Jerita Howard,
Peggy Sturrock, Patty Bowdoin, Virginia, and Ruby Shelton.*

to San Francisco through Golden Gate Baptist Theological
Seminary, and during a trip there they visited Jade and
Woodrow in their home. Talk turned to a trip to China. Ed
died before the trip could be planned, but Virginia signed up
for a tour led by the San Francisco couple in 1979.

When she returned, Virginia was interviewed for an
article in the *Abilene Reporter-News*. "On this second visit I
noticed how the people are quiet and polite, but also very
curious," she told reporter Pat Kilpatrick.[3] Virginia told the
reporter that she had visited China for the same reason she
went to Russia in 1976–for an education. Virginia recalled
how the tour group had flown on Russian planes and ridden
in Japanese buses during the China trip as they visited
museums, farming communes, hospitals, factories and craft
shops. Because of her medical background, Virginia was given
a look at the medical practices in China. She said she was

surprised to discover that 80 percent of the doctors there were women, but very few were surgeons.[4] As always, Virginia tied her journey to her Christian experience. She told the reporter that it would be difficult to present Christianity to the almost one billion people living in the country at that time. "How are we going to present Christianity to them in the proper way?" she asked. "If the only sign of Christ they see is through us, then we who go there have a burden to present Christ as He would have us" was her conclusion. She said she believes the Christian's approach to China would have to be a slow one to ensure presentation of Christianity in the proper light—one of humor, understanding, and concern.[5]

Virginia still has copies of *The Fifth Chinese Daughter* to hand out to people unfamiliar with Jade Snow Wong, who died in 2006. The book chronicles Wong's early life growing up in San Francisco in a traditional Chinese family. Virginia was impressed with Wong's life story and her accomplishments. Wong was a 1942 graduate of Mills College, a prestigious women's college in Oakland, California. An obituary in the *San Jose Mercury News* noted that in 1947 an enamel bowl sculpted by Wong was selected for the Museum of Modern Art's "100 Useful Objects of Fine Art." The author of the obituary, L.A. Chung, noted that Wong had one-woman shows from "Chicago to Karachi."[6] She was so highly thought of that she was featured in Bill Moyers's 2003 PBS special, *Becoming American: The Chinese Experience* and was the subject of a 1976 PBS documentary, *Jade Snow.* She also reviewed books for the *Los Angeles Times* and wrote a second memoir, *No Chinese Stranger.*[7] She also is among the entrants in the biography section of the National Women's History Project.[8]

Virginia would make one more trip to China. In 1983, she took her sister Ruth Williams, a granddaughter, Sundi Spivey, and grandson, Sid Roberts, who is now a physician in Lufkin. Also on the trip was Jaxie Short, who had been a missionary to China in the 1940s and was returning for the first time since 1949. Jaxie and two sisters, Eunice and Willene, all attended Oklahoma Baptist University. Jaxie graduated in 1936 and later received an alumni achievement award. In 2002, on the 92nd anniversary of Oklahoma Baptist University, the school's president, Dr. Mark Brister, spoke during a ceremony about people who had made a difference at the university. Among them were the Short sisters, whose father was a professor. "Each of them gave OBU something unique as they grew older. Eunice was a longtime administrator, Jaxie was a missionary to China, and Willene was a campus artist," Brister said in his remarks.[9]

At one time Jaxie had lived in Abilene and was a member of First Baptist Church, where she and Virginia met. Sid recalled that during the 1983 trip, Jaxie located people she knew from the time she had spent on the mission field in China. He also recalled how meaningful it was to him to be with a group of committed Christians and to see their influence. The group took Bibles to the Chinese and met with missionaries during their stay in China. "To me that was such an exciting time–seeing what God was doing in other places," Sid said.

Seeing what God was doing in other places, as well as next door, has been a central theme of Virginia's life, too. Not a day goes by that she doesn't see evidence of God at work in people's lives. And she relishes opportunities to share those revelations with others. She can't remember a time in her life, from childhood to the present, that she hasn't been tuned in to God's wonders. It started at home and at the family's Baptist church in Temple–a place that Virginia said she "never thought of not going." It continued at a Baptist college and First Baptist Church in Abilene, where today Virginia is as highly thought of as she was as a young college student and later as Abilene's first female physician. For Virginia, being a Baptist comes as naturally as breathing, or as she put it, "I could change the color of my eyes as quickly as I could change my faith."

BY LORETTA FULTON

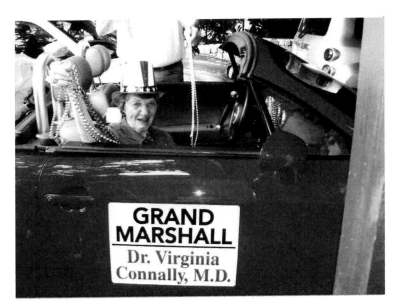

Virginia as grand marshal for a Fourth of July parade in 2007.

Virginia enterains a Sunday School class in her home.

BY LORETTA FULTON

Chapter 11
TAKING THE GOSPEL TO THE WORLD

"She may well be a Baptist saint."
∞ Dr. Walter B. Shurden, retired professor and executive
director of the Center for Baptist Studies, Mercer University

In John Pierce's 2009 article for *Baptists Today*, Virginia
related a memory from her youth about her upbringing. "I
remember my mother taking me to a window in our house
and saying in kind of a sad voice, 'If we don't take the gospel
to the whole world, we're going to regret it.'"[1] Those words
weren't lost on Virginia. She has been taking the gospel to the
whole world, from literal neighbors to global neighbors, ever
since. Although she did not become a vocational missionary
herself, Virginia has been an "everyday missionary" all her life.
She did participate in medical missions to Venezuela and took
Bibles to foreign lands, but on an everyday basis Virginia lives
the gospel in plain view of anyone who comes into contact
with her. Jack and Ann Griggs, whom Virginia met in the
1960s when Griggs' college roommate, Bill Petty, went to
work for Ed, recalled how Virginia became such an integral
part of their lives. At one time, Griggs left the presidency of
a bank in San Antonio to start a new bank in Dallas. Griggs
recalled that one day he got a check in the mail from Virginia
to purchase stock in the new bank. "She just wanted to be an
encouragement to us," he said. "I didn't even know she knew
I was starting a new bank."

In 1991, Griggs became dean of the College of Business
Administration at Abilene Christian University, and the family,
including four children, moved back to Abilene. Jack and Ann
recalled how Virginia sometimes spent Thanksgiving and
Christmas in their home. Once, Ann remembered, Virginia
looked at her and said, "Ann, how are you feeling?" Ann
replied that she wasn't feeling well at all, to which Virginia

responded, "Let me look at your throat." On the spot, Virginia prescribed some antibiotics that she had at her home. Jack was sent to get them. The couple grew so close to Virginia and were so influenced by her spirituality that she was the person they thought of for a special blessing. After celebrating an anniversary at a local restaurant, the couple decided they wanted a special way to mark the date. "We went over to Virginia's for her to give us a blessing," Jack recalled. "She prayed a special blessing for us." To this day, the couple cherishes the evening and the special part that Virginia played in it. "When we wanted to have a spiritual blessing, it wasn't a preacher or a priest we thought of," Jack said. "It was Virginia Connally."

Virginia joined Abilene's First Baptist Church in 1930, the year she enrolled in Simmons University. One of the first things she did when she returned as Dr. Virginia Boyd in 1940 was to renew old acquaintances and to once again embark on an active church life. First Baptist was a good choice for a woman of Virginia's pioneering spirit. The church had appointed a woman missionary, Blanche Rose Walker, in 1905, which was quite unusual for the time. When Virginia opened her practice, Walker was one of her first patients. With Virginia's status as one of three women in her medical school class at Louisiana State University and as Abilene's first female physician, it seemed only logical that she would one day break another barrier. It took some time—until 1997—but Virginia eventually became a deacon in a Baptist church, a feat that at one time seemed almost as impossible as a woman earning a medical degree. But by 1997, as with most of society, at least a faction of the Baptist church had changed. Although churches affiliated with the Southern Baptist Convention remain staunchly conservative, including views on women's roles in the church, more moderate Baptist churches have loosened the reins. In some Baptist churches, women even fill pulpits.

First Baptist Church in Abilene is affiliated with the Baptist General Convention of Texas, a much more moderate faction of the church than the Southern Baptist Convention, which

Virginia said, "went crazy" when fundamentalists took over the leadership. Hardin-Simmons University, Virginia's alma mater, also is supported by the BGCT. On Sunday, February 16, 1997, First Baptist Church in Abilene installed its first five women deacons, including Virginia. The women, along with six male deacons, were elected by the congregation to serve three-year terms. Another of the women deacons, Charlotte Bridges, recalled that to the women chosen as deacons, the election was merely procedure. "This is what we're already doing in a way," was the thinking of the new deacons, Bridges said. "We're just going to have a new name." But the election was much more significant than that and a few people even left the church over the election of women deacons. Bridges' husband, Dr. Julian Bridges, is a retired Hardin-Simmons University sociology professor and the couple has been friends with Virginia for years. In their eyes, Virginia fits the description of a person born to be a deacon. "She's very mission-minded," Charlotte Bridges said. "She really outshines everyone in many ways."

Virginia's current pastor, Dr. Phil Christopher, recalled that because the congregation knew of Virginia's servant life and her status as a "true matriarch of the church," controversy over the ordination of women deacons was minimal at First Baptist Church. "How could anyone object?" Christopher said. "Her life is a living testimony of what the role of deacon means. The word 'deacon' is not a noun or position, but a verb that means service. So if you look up the word 'service' in the dictionary, you will find a picture of Virginia."

David Leyerle can certainly vouch for that. He recalled that in 1978, Virginia took the initiative to go to Louisville, Kentucky, to meet the Leyerle family when David was considering a ministry position with First Baptist Church in Abilene. In the ensuing years, Leyerle worked both in recreation ministry with First Baptist's Family Life Center and later with the church's City Light Community Ministries. Leyerle saw Virginia's deacon heart up close and personal. "Dr. Connally is progressive and ecumenical in her Christian theology and action in carrying it out," he said. "She championed the cause for children regardless of their circumstances." He recalled visiting public housing complexes with Virginia and how she would kneel down to be at eye level with a child. When First Baptist started its City Light outreach program, Virginia bought a new 15-passenger van for the program and went with Leyerle to a bus auction to purchase two additional buses. "Dr. Connally is very quick to respond to both the need of the less fortunate and offer ways of encouragement to them," Leyerle said.

It's fortunate that Virginia's home church recognized her gifts and chose her to serve as a deacon. Virginia's love of the Baptist church runs deep and that is where she is committed to serve. As Christopher noted, she is committed to Baptist distinctives—the core values of the historic denomination. "She believes a person is free to choose and that you cannot coerce a person into believing," Christopher said. "She has deep concerns about the moral climate of our culture but still defends the cherished Baptist principle of separation of church and state." Christopher recalled the trip Virginia took to Providence, Rhode Island, in observance of the 400th anniversary of the Baptist church in America. Providence is the home of Roger Williams and the first Baptist church established in this country. As a knowledgeable historian, Virginia knows of—and appreciates—persecution that Baptist forefathers and foremothers endured to exercise their beliefs, Christopher noted. As usual, Virginia not only learned something from the experience, she was determined to share it with others, including her pastor. "She gave me a history of Roger Williams's church in Providence, signed by the author, that has a prominent place in my office," Christopher said.

Virginia's love of all things Baptist started as a child growing up in a Baptist home and attending a Baptist church and Sunday school. She was baptized at her home church in Temple about age 11 or 12, she recalled, and was an active participant in the Baptist Young People's Union. She stayed active in church after enrolling in college and remained a faithful churchgoer while enduring the rigors of being newly married and a pioneer female medical student in New Orleans. She even took on a challenge at First Baptist Church in Abilene that came as a surprise to her. When Genna was about 11 years old, a teacher was needed for her Sunday school class. Virginia volunteered, even though she had not liked the idea of being a teacher when she was in college. "I said I would do it for a few Sundays until they found someone," Virginia recalled. "Little did I know they weren't ever going to look for someone else." So Virginia stuck with the job and grew to enjoy it. She even drove her stately Rolls Royce to Hendrick Home for Children to pick up children for her class.

As the years passed, Virginia grew more involved with the larger Baptist church, eventually serving on the inaugural boards of Texas Baptist Missions Foundation and Texas Baptists Committed, a moderate organization that refers to itself as "mainstream Baptists of Texas." Dr. William M. Pinson Jr. first met Virginia when he was president of Golden Gate Theological Seminary in Mill Valley, California, from 1972 to 1982. From 1983 to 2000, he was executive director of the Baptist General Convention of Texas and got to know Virginia well during that time. Virginia still has the program from the dedication of a grand piano that she donated to Golden Gate while Pinson was there. Pinson said Virginia struck him as a person who was always very positive and "extraordinarily bright." He described her as a "hands-on doer and encourager and thinker–one of the most remarkable people I've ever known." Pinson recalled that in 1985, the Baptist General Convention of Texas under Pinson's leadership started Mission Texas. The goal was to establish 2,000 new churches in Texas, especially reaching out to the state's growing Hispanic population. "She pitched in and helped with that immediately," Pinson said.

Virginia always has been willing to pitch in and help, whether financially or hands-on. Because of her intellect and ability to analyze situations and make decisions, she was a popular addition to boards of directors, whether for Baptist organizations or other institutions. Her inquisitive mind and her sense of adventure naturally led her to take part in Baptist functions worldwide. A favorite over the years has been attending the Baptist World Alliance's Baptist World Congress, which is held every five years in a different part of the world. Baptist World Alliance is a global fellowship of Baptist conventions and unions. The 20th Baptist World Congress was held in July 2010 in Honolulu. Virginia did not attend the 2010 congress, but previous trips have taken her to Canada, Argentina, and England. It was on the 2005 trip to the Baptist World Congress in Birmingham, England, that Virginia met Dr. Walter B. Shurden and his wife, Kay Wilson Shurden. Immediately, two more lasting friendships were born. Virginia was so impressed with the Shurdens' knowledge and hospitality that she signed up for another trip with them in 2008 to visit the historic original Baptist church in America that Christopher referred to. Virginia still speaks glowingly of the Shurdens, and they, in turn, were equally impressed with Virginia.

Walter Shurden was the founding executive director of the Center for Baptist Studies at Mercer University in Macon, Georgia. Now retired, he carries the title of "Minister at Large, Mercer University." In addition to working as executive director of the Center for Baptist Studies, Shurden also was the Callaway Professor of Christianity in the Roberts Department of Christianity at the university and was chairman of the department for seven years. Prior to going to Mercer in 1983, among his other achievements, Shurden was a professor of church history from 1976 to 1983 and dean of the School of Theology from 1980 to 1983 at The Southern Baptist Theological Seminary in Louisville, Kentucky. In other words, Shurden is well-versed in Baptist history and theology, both appealing to Virginia. Kay Shurden also possesses traits that Virginia admires. Kay Shurden said she became a feminist while attending graduate school at the University of Tennessee in her late 30s. "When I met Virginia," Kay Shurden said, "I realized she had become a feminist, someone who sees herself as a person of worth and value and has gifts to give outside her role as a wife and mother, long before most others had come to that realization. She was kind and gentle, yet determined and focused, both feminine and feminist."

Shurden said she was impressed that Virginia seemed unaware of how unusual she is in this world "where women often become strident and demanding in their search for rights and privileges, a world in which it is difficult to find a place for our gifts and abilities." Shurden said she immediately became attached to Virginia, who "reached out to me in love and acceptance." She found Virginia to be a woman who is appreciative of the past and open to the future, someone who is open to learning from as many different experiences as possible. "I found her to be one of a kind, a woman both self-assured and humble, a true Christian feminist," Shurden said. "A truly loving person is a work of art."

Walter Shurden was equally impressed with Virginia's personal qualities, her intellect and accumulated knowledge. On the trip to England in 2005 for the Baptist World Congress, the Shurdens were co-hosts along with Dr. Drayton Sanders. "I know no other way to describe Virginia Connally other than she is a delight" Shurden said. "Intellectually curious and spiritually sensitive, she has appeared to me to be a person who loves relationships and contacts with people." Like his wife, Kay, Walter Shurden said he felt a closeness to Virginia almost immediately. Shurden said he had no doubt Virginia was a fine physician in her day "because of her love for people." He said he also appreciates how financially generous Virginia is when it comes to supporting causes she believes in. Shurden also picked up on Virginia's love of the Baptist church and its missions. He was so impressed, in fact, that he was the one who suggested to John Pierce that he profile Virginia for *Baptists Today* in 2009. "She may well be a Baptist saint," Shurden surmised.

Virginia as member of the board of trustees at Hardin-Simmons University in 1985. With her from left are Bailey Stone, Gene Adams, Morey Millerman, and Dr. Jesse C. Fletcher, president at the time.

Virginia visits with Keith and Helen Jean Parks at a meeting of the Southern Baptist Convention Foreign Mission Board in Richmond, Virginia

BY LORETTA FULTON

Chapter 12
ALWAYS MISSION-MINDED

"I never got away from the idea Virginia planted."
∞ Helen Jean Parks, retired missionary,
along with husband, Keith Parks

No one who knows Virginia would argue her qualifications for sainthood. One woman who learned of Virginia's saintly qualities early in life was Helen Jean Bond Parks, who was supported by the Connallys while serving in the mission field in Indonesia, along with her husband, Keith Parks. Long before Helen Jean was "Mrs. Parks" or a missionary, she encountered Virginia. Helen Jean's father, Dr. W.D. Bond, was an English professor at Hardin-Simmons University, Virginia's alma mater. Helen Jean entered the university in 1944, just four years after Virginia opened her office. She earned a degree in English, with minors in music and journalism, in 1948. She recalled that during her early years at the university, she suffered a seemingly endless number of colds, coughs, and congestion. "So my mother announced to me that she was taking me to see a new ENT in town, the first woman physician in Abilene," Parks recalled. "Her coming back to Abilene was causing quite a buzz."

Parks said she was impressed with this "pretty, efficient, personable doctor–dressed in crisp white uniform–as she checked my nose and throat." Then Virginia asked her young patient an unusual question–"Do you eat breakfast?" Parks said she suspected that "no" would be the wrong answer and hurriedly tried to form a noncommittal reply. Before she could utter a response, her mother answered for her, "No, she doesn't." Virginia, always on top of the latest studies, had her answer ready for that suspected response, Parks recalled. "Well," Virginia said, "studies show that college women have the worst diet in the U.S. So this is your main problem. I want you to start eating breakfast–every morning! No excuses, understand?" Parks remembered vividly her introduction to Virginia, who became not only her physician, but also her "mentor, patron, sponsor, Christian role model, friend, and confidante–one of the most important persons in my life." Indeed, Virginia would become an integral part of the lives of Helen Jean and Keith Parks as they entered the mission field together. Virginia, in addition to having a keen medical mind, also had a keen insight into people, often seeming to know more about them than they knew about themselves. Such was the case with her young patient. Parks recalled that as a senior at Hardin-Simmons, she was chairperson of the annual Religious Focus Week. Feeling called to vocational Christian service, she responded to an invitation during a student chapel service at the end of the special week.

She recalled that on the following Sunday, her pastor at First Baptist Church, Dr. Jesse Northcutt, asked students who had made decisions at the university to share those with the congregation. "As members filed by to speak to those of us in line, Virginia beamed as she took my hand. 'Are you going to be a missionary?' she asked. "Oh, no, ma'am, I am going to do youth or student work!" Parks actually did go on to do some youth and student work but eventually became a missionary, just as Virginia had seemed to know. At the time, though, "I had not even thought about missions and was frankly horrified by the thought," Parks said. "But I never got away from the idea Virginia planted." Not only did Virginia plant the seed, she also cultivated it and watched with pleasure as the seedling took hold and blossomed. Helen Jean Bond married Keith Parks in 1952, and he taught at Hardin-Simmons in the 1953-1954 school year, while completing his doctor of theology dissertation from Southwestern Baptist Theological Seminary in Fort Worth, Texas, about 150 miles east of Abilene. Not only did Parks teach a full load of freshman Bible and homiletics courses during that time, he also pastored a small Baptist church about 100 miles north of Abilene. Virginia married Ed Connally in 1953 and the couples got to know each other.

Eventually, Keith and Helen Jean were appointed missionaries to Indonesia. Virginia was seeing her prophesy come true and took an active role in the couple's lives, from financial support to a car to use while on furlough in the United States to the latest in U.S. innovations—a box of strawberry-flavored corn flakes. The financial support came first. One day a letter arrived in Indonesia from Dr. Elwyn Skiles, who at the time was pastor of First Baptist Church in Abilene. He informed the Parkses that a couple in the church who wished to remain anonymous had made arrangements through the Southern Baptist Convention's Foreign Missions Board to "adopt" Helen Jean and pay her basic salary through the board. "Much later we learned they were Ed and Virginia," Helen Jean Parks said. On another occasion, the couple got notice from the local post office in Semarang, Central Java, Indonesia, that a package was being held from them, pending a customs fee of twenty dollars. "When we checked on it," Parks recalled, "we were shocked that it was a box of strawberry-flavored corn flakes from the Connallys sent airmail at a cost of twenty U.S. dollars!"

As was customary in Indonesia, the couple engaged in haggling, telling customs officers the package was merely breakfast cereal and that it was not worth more than two dollars. If the customs officials insisted on charging twenty dollars, then they could just return the package to the Connallys. A back-and-forth exchange ensued. "They finally relented and let us have it for a fee of five dollars," Parks recalled. The thought of the Connallys deciding to mail a box of cereal delighted the Parkses as much as the strawberry-flavored novelty itself. Helen Jean recalled her husband saying, "I can just picture Ed and Virginia eating a bowl of this new cereal and saying, 'We bet Keith and Helen Jean would enjoy this!'" And, indeed, they did. Leave it to Ed and Virginia, though, to top even that totally unexpected gift. As Keith and Helen Jean prepared to leave for their first furlough back to the United States, they received another letter from their home pastor, Dr. Elwyn Skiles. He wrote that a couple at the church, once

Longtime friend, the late Agnes Beckham, and a missionary couple visit with Virginia at First Baptist Church.

again wishing to remain anonymous, would be providing a car for their use while on leave. Shortly after arriving in Abilene, the Parkses spoke at First Baptist Church and afterward stood at the front so that people could come by to greet them. "Walking outside we saw this new be-ribboned automobile parked on the sidewalk," Helen Jean recalled. As members filed by, the Parkses kept wondering who their "Santa Claus" was. And then it was obvious, Helen Jean said. "At the very end of the line were Ed and Virginia, looking like "the cat that swallowed the canary. Their secret was apparent!"

The relationship between Virginia and Keith and Helen Jean Parks grew deep, not just because of the obvious chemistry, shared interests, and admiration. It also involved theology and monumental changes within the Southern Baptist Convention. Virginia had been aligned with the SBC from her earliest days as a Baptist. But that ended when fundamentalists took over the convention leadership. Keith Parks, a career missionary, was elected president of the SBC's Foreign Mission Board in 1980 and would serve for 13 years. According the book, *The Fundamentalist Takeover in the Southern Baptist Convention: A Brief History*, during Parks' tenure, the FMB entered forty new countries to give the FMB 3,918 missionaries in 126 countries.[1] The book noted that as early as 1985 Parks "spoke out courageously to contend that the controversy in the denomination was damaging Southern Baptist mission efforts," describing SBC missionaries as "hostages" to the conflict. But, according to the book, the "takeover" group continued to question the biblical orthodoxy of some missionaries.[2] Parks had said he wanted to remain president of the Foreign Mission Board until 1995. But after years of trying to please fundamentalist trustees, Parks announced in March 1992 that he would retire in October that year.[3] A month after leaving the FMB, Parks joined the Cooperative Baptist Fellowship as missions coordinator. Dr. William M. Pinson Jr., Executive Director of the Baptist General Convention of Texas at the time, said Parks "helped Southern Baptists realize the extent of the world's lostness."[4] And, according to the authors of *The Fundamentalist Takeover in the Southern Baptist Convention: A Brief History*, "That worldwide vision was now being put to work on behalf of a more moderate community of Southern Baptists who were seeking a missions program they could support in good conscience."[5]

Virginia is, and always has been, a part of the "moderate community," having little use for fundamentalist views. Their tightly held beliefs and refusal to entertain other thoughts goes directly against Virginia's grain. "If you don't believe like they do, you're out" is her complaint against fundamentalists. "I've always been with groups that were in opposition to them." Virginia is very much a thinker, which inevitably involves theology for her. But she also is very much a doer, a woman who acts on those deep, wise, and insightful thoughts. Since much of her thinking involves theology and the church, it stands to reason that much of her action would follow suit. Whether the theology is embedded in actions such as paying the way for a missionary or displayed more actively like taking on a mission trip herself, it is the bedrock of all that Virginia does.

Even though as children Virginia and her sister Ruth envisioned becoming missionaries if anything happened to their parents, that would not be the path Virginia would take. She always has supported mission efforts financially and by serving on boards, purchasing a home for missionaries in Abilene while on furlough, and by giving personal support and encouragement to people like Keith and Helen Jean Parks. But earlier in her life she also participated in several short-term medical missions. When Virginia was honored in 1988 with one of the first Pathfinder Awards given by the YWCA and the *Abilene Reporter-News*, she had recently taken part in a medical mission trip to Venezuela. The trip was sponsored by the Joint Tennessee-Venezuela Partnership. In an article in the *Reporter-News*, Virginia noted that the medical team saw 10,000 patients in six days. In addition to serving medical needs, the team heard 800 professions of faith, including two Venezuelan doctors. In the article, Virginia said an evangelistic team followed the medical mission and that 2,000 more decisions for Christ resulted. Virginia's assessment of the trip: "Research and religion…it's very rewarding."

That mission trip was one of three that Virginia took to Venezuela. Another came in 1992 and was sponsored by the Southern Baptist Convention's Foreign Mission Board, as it was known then. Among the 134-member volunteer medical team were several from Abilene and the surrounding area. Virginia, Dr. James L. Tucker Jr., and his daughter, Maggie Nugent, Dr. George Dawson and his wife, Dorothy, who was a registered nurse, made up the Abilene contingent. In 1987, Dawson had purchased land at 1210 North Eighteenth Street to build a clinic. That also happened to be the former location of the home of Virginia's uncle, Dr. W.R. Snow, where Virginia lived while attending college. The Dawsons and Virginia got to know one another when the Dawsons settled in Abilene in 1959. Dawson had been stationed at Dyess Air Force Base and left the service on July 4, 1959. After opening his original practice at 1200 North Mockingbird Lane, Dawson began attending monthly staff meetings at Hendrick Memorial Hospital and the local medical society. He met Virginia there and later the couples got better acquainted at church. Dawson recalled sending patients with eye problems to Virginia. Dorothy taught a Sunday school class at Hendrick's children's hospital while her husband was making rounds. She remembered asking one little boy if he had ever been to Sunday school before, to which he enthusiastically replied "Yes, ma'am, and I went in a Rolls Royce!" referring to Virginia's car.

The Dawsons also recalled another simple act of thoughtfulness and kindness that so characterizes Virginia. The Dawsons were acquainted with Helen Jean Parks' mother and stopped by one day to visit. They noticed a vase of roses and asked if it were her birthday. "No," she replied, it's Helen Jean's birthday but Virginia Connally always sends me roses on Helen Jean's birthday." At the time, Helen Jean was serving as a missionary in Indonesia, and the remembrance was greatly appreciated by her mother. On another occasion, when George Dawson was serving on the Southern Baptist Convention's Foreign Mission Board, Virginia attended an FMB meeting in Richmond, Virginia. Afterward, they drove to another city and everybody knew Virginia and was happy to see her, Dawson recalled. "They kept talking about the piano," Dawson said, and Virginia, apparently forgetting her act of generosity, said, "Do you think I gave them that piano?" And she was—and still is—just as generous at home. The Dawsons recalled an occasion when they were playing dominoes at the Abilene Woman's Club. Each table had a bouquet of flowers as a table setting. To no one's surprise, Virginia had provided them.

Virginia's skills and commitment as a physician matched her generous spirit, the Dawsons recalled. The mission trips sponsored by the SBC's Foreign Mission Board consisted of teams of physicians, nurses, pharmacists, nutritionists, and other caregivers. George Dawson recalled that Virginia ran an eye clinic during a mission trip to Venezuela in 1992. Dawson remembered that the clinic operated out of an air-conditioned downtown building and that lines would start forming at 3:30 a.m. in anticipation of the clinic's opening. "Virginia would be there at 7 o'clock in the morning and worked until 7 o'clock at night," Dawson said. "Her stamina—to be on her feet that long—always amazed me." That particular trip was remarkable, not only for the work performed by the team members, but also for a disaster that the volunteers narrowly escaped. The missions team left Venezuela just 15 hours before an attempted coup in which about 60 people were killed and hundreds were injured, according to an account of the trip in the March 14, 1992, edition of the *Abilene Reporter-News*.[6] A team member, Franciene Johnson of Haskell, said in the article that a missionary who had accompanied the mission volunteers to the Caracas airport got caught in the crossfire on his way back home but was not injured. "We saw so many ways that the Lord took care of us," Johnson was quoted as saying. "That was just the last one." Johnson told *Reporter-News* Religion Editor Roy A. Jones II that she and her husband, Elbert Johnson, had just gotten home to Haskell when they heard a television report about the attempted coup. "We just said a prayer of thanksgiving and prayed for the missionaries and for the new friends we'd left behind—especially the new Christians," she said.[7]

BY LORETTA FULTON

Virginia makes notes on the long flight home from her eighth trip to Finland in September 2010

Chapter 13
LOOKING OUTWARD

*"She always sees that the mission of the church is
to look outward and not inward."*
∞ Dr. Phil Christopher, pastor,
First Baptist Church, Abilene, Texas

Two of Virginia's enduring loves have been missions
and her alma mater, Hardin-Simmons University. She found
numerous ways to serve both, including working with the
Texas Baptist Missions Foundation and establishing the
Connally Missions Center at Hardin-Simmons. Being
mission-minded is a natural for Virginia, her pastor, Dr. Phil
Christopher, believes, because she has a global perspective.
"She always sees that the mission of the church is to look
outward and not inward," he said. Christopher noted that
Virginia was a part of the leadership that moved First Baptist
to conduct a $5 million campaign for missions. "Virginia
understands that missions is caring for the needs of children
in our own community, helping children read, providing
clean water in Third World countries, or building bridges
in Muslim countries," Christopher said. A Bible verse that
Christopher believes best describes Virginia's understanding
of missions is from the book of Isaiah. It is the text that Jesus
used in his first sermon at Nazareth: "The Spirit of the Lord
is upon me, because he has anointed me to preach good news
to the poor. He has sent me to proclaim freedom for the
prisoners and recovery of the sight of the blind and to release
the oppressed." Virginia's prayer, Christopher noted, has always
been "open the eyes of our hearts to the needs around us."
The Texas Baptist Missions Foundation, a part of the
Baptist General Convention of Texas, started in 1984 with
Bill Arnold as president. That same year Arnold, who still is
the only president to ever serve the Foundation, met Virginia.

Before too many years had passed, Arnold noticed that Virginia had a propensity for saying to people, "God sent you to me today." In 1992, the Foundation appointed its first advisory board, and Arnold immediately thought of Virginia to be a founding board member. Indeed, it seemed God had put the two together in 1984 for a reason. Today, Virginia is a board member emeritus of the Foundation. Another Abilenian bearing that distinction is Eunice Chambless, for whom a hospitality house is named that serves family members of men incarcerated at the two state prisons in Abilene. While Virginia was still active on the board, Arnold saw her heart for missions at work. He saw that she was sensitive to the needs of others. "She really hurts for people in need," Arnold said. Another trait that Arnold still admires in Virginia is her ability to see and appreciate strengths in others that she might not have herself. And she doesn't hesitate to say so. "She is a great encourager," Arnold said.

Not only did Virginia serve ably as a member of the advisory board for a number of years, she also was one of the first to jump on board the idea of Mission Texas, a plan set forth by the Foundation to plant 2,000 new churches in Texas between 1985 and 1990. Just as Dr. William M. Pinson Jr., executive director of the BGCT at the time had recalled, Arnold remembered Virginia's enthusiasm for the endeavor. "She was really committed to helping us accomplish that," Arnold said. She was so committed, in fact, that after the first 1,000 church plants were set in motion, the Foundation named "God's 200" to finish the work. Virginia was one of the 200 who committed to providing the resources needed to start five churches each.

Virginia also made numerous commitments to good works closer to home. An opportunity to support both her love of missions and her alma mater came in 1991 when Dr. Lanny Hall was selected for his first stint as president of Hardin-Simmons University. Hall would work ten years in that position before being named chancellor in 2001. In 2003, he became president of a sister Baptist institution, Howard Payne

University in Brownwood, Texas. In 2009, the universities, located about 75 miles apart, swapped administrators when Hall was hired as president of Hardin-Simmons for the second time and Dr. William (Bill) Ellis, provost and chief academic officer at Hardin-Simmons, was named president of Howard Payne.

In 1991, when Hall first was selected president of Hardin-Simmons, the Connally Chair of Missions was in its third year. In 1981, Virginia had funded the Connally Endowed Professorship of Missions, which was upgraded to a chair in 1988. When Hall came aboard in 1991, one of the first people he heard from was Virginia. True to her reputation, she sent a handwritten note welcoming Hall as the new president of her alma mater. Hall already was familiar with the Connally name and legacy. "I was impressed with her history," Hall said.

One of the first things Hall had noticed when he arrived on campus was an unattractive spot on an otherwise stately and charming campus. He had an idea for transforming that eyesore into something beautiful and lasting. And, he had an idea for how to achieve that transformation. Hall and his wife, Carol, took Virginia to dinner, where he laid out his idea. He envisioned a new building dedicated to missions. A place where pastors and visiting missionaries could meet. A place that student groups such as the Baptist Student Ministries could call home. The Halls took Virginia to the spot he had in mind. "This is where we would like to build a missions center," Hall told Virginia. He had spoken the magic word, "missions," and Virginia was on board. That was the easy part. The hard part came in persuading Virginia that the building should bear the Connally name. "We had to work on her for that," Hall recalled. But it all came to pass and the building was dedicated in 2000. The Connally Missions Center constantly is abuzz with students, pastors, faculty, and missionaries sharing stories and ideas and gaining insight in the mission field. Hall frequently sees Virginia, either on campus or at Baptist functions. Wherever she goes, she draws a crowd because people are eager to hear her words of wisdom. "People know who she is and they have great respect for her," Hall said.

Hall's immediate predecessor, Dr. Jesse C. Fletcher, came to Hardin-Simmons in 1977. Prior to that, he had served 15 years with the Foreign Mission Board of the Southern Baptist Convention. By the time he arrived in Abilene, Fletcher was well aware of Virginia's reputation and legacy at Hardin-Simmons, and he sought her out. "Virginia was high on my radar screen by the time I got here," he said. Fletcher was president of the university until 1991. He then served as chancellor until 2001 and was interim president in 2009 before Hall came on board. Fletcher now holds the title of president emeritus and was the first holder of the Connally Chair of Missions. One of the first moves Fletcher made when he became president in 1977 was to ask Virginia to be on the board of trustees. He recalled that she was an active board member and one who was "spiritually articulate." When she spoke, people listened, Fletcher recalled. "I don't think Virginia ever had to worry about an audience," he said.

Since people tended to listen to what Virginia had to say, she was an ideal person to help with fundraising efforts. Fletcher, a licensed pilot, arranged a one-day flying trip to visit with potential donors in El Paso, San Antonio, and Houston. Even by air, that's a considerable chunk of Texas to cover in one day. But the entourage, which included the chairman of HSU's board of trustees, Virginia, and others, made it in a spectacular fashion. In that one day, the HSU ambassadors raised $2.5 million for the university. Virginia's persistence and stamina were two traits admired by many who knew her, including Fletcher. During their years of service together at Hardin-Simmons, both of them used the facilities at First Baptist Church's Family Life Center for exercise. Fletcher recalled one day he was jogging and felt a faster runner coming up from behind. "I moved over to let this 'young person' pass," he said, "and it was Virginia lapping me." Just as Virginia showed persistence and stamina on the running track, she also carried those traits with her professionally. Fletcher recalled that when Virginia retired

Virginia at Baptist World Alliance meeting in Toronto in 1979.

from her medical practice in 1982, she didn't "quit." Instead, she found new avenues for her skills, intellect, and insights. In 1984, Virginia became the medical director and senior vice president of HSU's Fairleigh Dickinson Science Research Center, serving until the center closed in 1989. The center, constructed in 1981 by Fairleigh Dickinson Jr., was located on Ambler Avenue across from the HSU campus. According to a centennial history of Hardin-Simmons written by A. Yvonne Stackhouse, the center eventually housed a staff of 14 scientists, led by chief scientist John H. Brewer. [1] According to the book, in the early 1980s, the center undertook an ambitious project in immunodiagnostic testing. The projected included completing tests for ten different allergies which could be discovered through one blood sample from a patient. The center had a total of eight patents issued and several more pending.[2] Virginia and Brewer remained friends long after the center closed. She still has on her coffee table a wooden bowl on a pewter pedestal that Brewer handcrafted. More often than not, the bowl will be filled with nuts or candies for guests to enjoy.

Virginia's involvement with Hardin-Simmons University and her contributions to her alma mater have spanned most of her life. She has been cited by the university with four specific honors—the Distinguished Alumna Award in 1973, the Keeter Alumni Service Award in 1981, an Honorary Doctor of Humanities Degree in 1989, and induction into the HSU Hall of Leaders in 2004. The citation that was read during the Hall of Leaders induction ceremony noted that Virginia enrolled in Temple Junior College in 1929 amidst the turmoil of the Great Depression. From there, life didn't get easier. "At a time when pursuing a career in the medical profession for women was almost unheard of," the citation stated, "Virginia courageously, and with a heart determined to serve people with the gifts God had given her, set out to pursue a career in medicine. Despite discouragement from all fronts—from professors, deans, end even one family member—she entered Louisiana State University School of Medicine in 1933 and graduated in 1937 with the M.D. degree."[3] From there, Virginia served an internship and residency at Charity Hospital in New Orleans until 1940, when she left for Abilene to open her practice. The Hall of Leaders induction citation noted that Virginia "has repeatedly demonstrated, beyond measure, the true servant heart. She has given not only to this institution, but to many other worthy causes in Abilene and in missions. Her focus is always outward, never on herself. When informed in 1989 that she had been selected to receive an honorary doctorate from HSU, she replied, 'I hope that you have not made a mistake…I cannot possibly see how I qualify for this great honor. Hardin-Simmons has been so generous to me, so encouraging, so nourishing. It is I who should be giving this school, its president, and former presidents, the dedicated professors, and staff a very special honor.'"[4]

In addition to the four university honors, Virginia added to her list of "firsts" on February 22, 2011, when the Round

Table organization at Hardin-Simmons honored her with its inaugural Virtue Award, so named for Proverbs 31:10, which begins with the familiar words, "Who can find a virtuous woman? for her price is far above rubies." The award, with the Proverb inscribed on a lovely purple vase, was presented at the Round Table's centennial luncheon. At the conclusion of the luncheon, Round Table President Nancy Jones said the Virtue Award would be given to a woman who has shown exemplary leadership in her field, support to the university, and who represents Christian values and beliefs fundamental to Hardin-Simmons. Noting many of Virginia's achievements and connections to the university, Jones presented her with the award and said, "I am so proud to present the Virtue Award to the only logical choice, Dr. Virginia Boyd Connally."

The 2004 Hall of Leaders induction citation also noted Virginia's involvement over the years in the community, including being active in such diverse organizations as the Abilene Woman's Club, Hospice of Abilene, Pastoral Care and Counseling Center, Hendrick Foundation Board, the YWCA, Junior League of Abilene, Abilene Preservation League, Abilene Philharmonic Association, and the Big Country Audubon Society. When Virginia was awarded the inaugural Legacy Award from the Abilene Woman's Club in April 2009, an article in the *Abilene Reporter-News* noted that among her numerous "emeritus" titles was "trustee emeritus" of the Alliance for Women & Children, formerly the YWCA in Abilene. Kristina Jones, who was executive director of the organization at the time, said in the newspaper article that Virginia was one of the Alliance's biggest advocates. Jones remembered that when she first started work, Virginia was one of the first to congratulate her. "She was the one who came by to say 'welcome' before I could even call her." That trait is well known to the people fortunate to have crossed paths with Virginia. A friend, Debbie Blake, recalled that when she and her husband, John, moved into a new house across Sayles Boulevard from Virginia, it wasn't long before they heard from their new neighbor. "She sent me a note

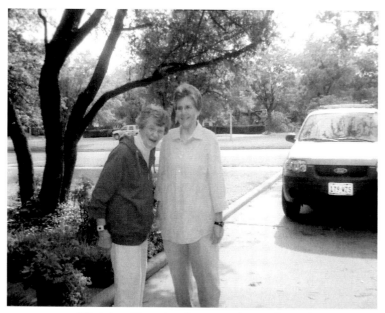

Virginia with author Loretta Fulton in front of
Virginia's home in Abilene.

telling me about herself and a flower arrangement welcoming me to the neighborhood," Blake said. "We've become best friends since."

Jones recalled in the *Reporter-News* article that butterfly pins were distributed at a luncheon when the name change to Alliance for Women & Children was announced. The story reported that Virginia ordered more pins and gave them away to friends and new acquaintances to show support for the name change and new affiliation, a move that wasn't popular with everyone. "For over a year, you would see her wearing a butterfly," Jones said in the article.[5] Being supportive is a trademark of Virginia. Whether routinely filling her table at the Abilene Woman's Club with luncheon guests or buying numerous tickets to local events to give to friends, Virginia finds ways to show her support. Love, compassion, and caring are in her soul and will be forever. At age 98, Virginia has earned the right to slow down, rest, and just "sit on the sidelines." But that is not Virginia. As long as she is able, she will be a player—"No sitting on the sidelines," as Lillian Johnson, Virginia's longtime personal assistant, puts it. "She impacts all those she meets. She feels a need to reach out and do what she can to help, whether it's advice or encouragement—just feeling a need of others." Typical of Virginia, she has found good in the aging processes that some people use as an excuse. As Lillian puts it, "She's not done yet making an impact on this world." Even though Virginia is still quite active, she acknowledges spending a little more time thinking, praying, and reflecting, or in her words, "As my life ebbs out, my hearing is going, my vision is going, and my thought processes are slowing—because of that, I have more time in solitude and time to reflect."

Reflection has been a hallmark of Virginia's life. She recalled that during her career, she sometimes would hear a female patient say, "You know, I always wanted to be a doctor." Virginia's initial reaction was to think, "You never did anything about it." But upon further reflection, she was sympathetic, realizing that unlike her, perhaps the woman never had been encouraged to pursue her dream. And, typical of Virginia, she didn't just have that thought. She acted on it—and still does. "It makes me realize how important it is to encourage, not to put people down," she said. To this day, anyone who has spent just a few minutes with Virginia can vouch for her determination to be just that—an encourager. That is one of Virginia's many virtues appreciated by her pastor, Dr. Phil Christopher, who came to First Baptist Church in 1995. Christopher recalled that one Sunday Virginia attached to her offering a small piece of paper with the message, "Phil, I will not be in Abilene on Easter Sunday. Service today was so inspiring. Love, Virginia." Christopher noted that Virginia was a great encourager to every pastor she had known at the church. She had the ability not to compare but to appreciate the unique gifts of each, Christopher remarked. One of Christopher's cherished notes from Virginia reads, "Thanks a million for being my pastor and friend." Thank you, too, for the inspiration and challenge that you constantly present."

Those comments give a quick overview of some of the values Virginia holds most dear–relationships, spirituality, and intellectual challenge. Christopher recognized Virginia's intellectual prowess right away after coming to First Baptist Church and still is reminded of her love of learning with every new book she sends him and note she leaves for him. Christopher said one of his greatest treasures is a book Virginia gave him, *The Sacrament of the Present Moment* by Jean-Pierre De Caussade and translated by Kitty Muggeridge, wife of Malcolm Muggeridge, whom Virginia and friends visited in England. The book reflects Virginia's approach to life, Christopher said. "Virginia sees each moment as sacred–if only all of us could see the holiness of each moment." Virginia's readings, of course, span decades and an expansive list of authors. Virginia read *The Shack*, a Christian novel written in 2007, and sent a review of it to her pastor. She agreed with the reviewer, who thought the book could impact a younger generation like Bunyan's *Pilgrim's Progress* had impacted her when she read it at age sixteen. "I can only wonder how many sixteen-year-olds read *Pilgrim's Progress*," Christopher said, "yet, being a 'pilgrim on the journey' is the way that she has lived her life. This is a parable of her life. She is a pilgrim–a pioneer and not a settler."

Virginia may see her life as "ebbing out" but those who are close to her, as well as new people she encounters, still see a vibrant personality, a keen and inquisitive mind, and the heart of a saint. She is so active, in fact, that she still meets with the quilting club at the Abilene Woman's Club, even though she doesn't quilt. It's enough for her to greet a new day by scurrying off to the Woman's Club to enjoy conversation with her longtime friends in the quilting club–Carol Hall, Patty Taliaferro, Tina Hunter, Gloria McDaniel, Mary Wright, Bobbie Gee, Lenore Waldrop, Virginia Nollner, Era Jo Lester, Dottie Korman, Dolores Shaw, Peggy Teague, Norma Schaffer, Helen Propst, and Lila Senter.

No one knows Virginia's saintly heart better than her pastor, Phil Christopher. From his unique perspective,

Christopher made the following observation: "Virginia lives a life of gratitude. Allow me to go back to the book that Virginia gave me, *The Sacrament of the Present Moment.* Every day for her is a gift. The people in her life are gifts that are to be treasured. I think of the words of the Apostle Paul, 'Let us not live like the foolish but the wise making the most of every opportunity.' Virginia makes the most of every opportunity. She once wrote me, 'Every tour, trip, effort, I wonder if this will be my last and ultimate? Only God knows. And this is enough.' It was enough for Virginia to be given the gift of another day and knowing that if this day was the last day, it would have been enough. For some people it is never enough—whatever they are given. For Virginia it was always enough because she lives in the present and sees life and her blessings as a gracious gift. She signed that note that she wrote to me early in the morning, 'Good morning, a good day to you, V. Connally. Enough.'

It has always been enough for Virginia, not wanting more but praising, 'This is the day that the Lord hath made; let us rejoice and be glad in it.'"

FAMILY GEMS

In December 2010, Virginia was treated to a variety of gatherings celebrating her 98th birthday. Some family members attending contributed a special memory of Virginia for inclusion in this book.

Mary Beth Geiger

My cousin Virginia was a part of my life before I was born. She and two other cousins were living with my family, which was my mother and dad (her Aunt Mae and Uncle Will), my two brothers and one sister while going to Hardin-Simmons. My mother was expecting me and had severe breathing problems. Virginia was one of the ones who helped her through that time with her adrenalin shots both before and after I was born. After Virginia graduated from medical school in New Orleans, she came back to Abilene as the first woman physician. I then got my first pair of glasses from her. The glasses were so revealing to me as to the world around me. I told my mother when I first got them, "Look, they put a sign on top of the Wooten Hotel."

Virginia has remained a part of my life ever since. We have treasured the time with her. She is an avid reader, so in turn has so much knowledge about many things. Reading, which was instilled in her by my mother, has been an important part of her life. Talking with her is always fun because of her many interests. At 98 she is still the interesting person I have enjoyed during my life. We span a time frame of the youngest and oldest cousins in our lives. That is special to me to have Virginia as my cousin.

Cheryl Tomasi Connally

In 1986, my husband Bill (Ed's grandson, Bill Connally) and I were moving from Pflugerville, Texas, to San Diego, Calif. We were driving out and spent our first night in Abilene so we could visit with Virginia. We got up very early the next morning to get a lot of miles under our belt. It was on this trip that I had my first true "box" lunch. Virginia found two small brown boxes and proceeded to make us each a lunch for the road of pimento cheese sandwiches, nuts, and other little items to fill that box. She also gave us advice to say "I love you" every day and a small book. It's been 24 years, but I still smile when I think of that little box of goodies.

(In a subsequent e-mail, Cheryl noted that she and her husband now live in New Hampshire. "I regret that we haven't been able to spend enough time with Virginia over the years...I treasure and save each handwritten note. Our son Jack, 16, is drawn to her as well. He sat right next to her during the sing-a-long."

Susan Cotten

My Mom is Mary Beth (Snow) Geiger, who is a first cousin of Dr. Virginia. I think that makes me a first cousin once-removed to Virginia. My husband, Mike, and I live in Commerce, Texas, and retired in August 2007. We are Harley riders and one of our first long distance trips, which we call our "Retirement Ride," was to a motorcycle rally in Ruidoso, New Mexico. We planned to stop in Abilene on our way west, so contacted Dr. Virginia to see if we could see her and she graciously offered for us to stay at her home. We arrived at her house on Sayles Boulevard mid-afternoon in September 2007 with the Harley pipes roaring. She was so kind and sweet to us, even had some friends come over to see her Harley family, then took us on a tour of Abilene (in her Lexus, not on the Harleys). The three of us stayed up into the wee hours of the night talking about every subject you could imagine, including political discussions between Virginia and my very conservative husband! We have been able to visit with Dr. Virginia once a year since that trip, and loved being able to share in her 98th birthday party!

Debbie Connally Driffill

I have many fond memories of Aunt Virginia and Uncle Ed. They visited us many times in San Antonio and we came to Abilene to visit them. I loved their home on Sayles Boulevard. It was a treat to eat breakfast outside on the patio and to go shopping, just Aunt Virginia and us four girls.

After the death of our grandfather, J.R. Connally, Jr., Aunt Virginia and Uncle Ed treated us just like we were their own grandchildren.

I will always be grateful to Aunt Virginia for her recommendation to help me get accepted to the first Dental Hygiene Class at the University of Texas Health Science Center at San Antonio. Competition was steep with 450 applicants and they only accepted 48. I have been practicing dental hygiene for 32 years and I thank Aunt Virginia for all she did to help me.

I will always have a special place in my heart for this unique and special lady. I want to thank Aunt Virginia and Genna again for the honor of inviting us to spend the weekend celebrating her 98th birthday.

NOTES

CHAPTER ONE

1   *Abilene Reporter-News*, September 22, 1940.

2   Drexel University College of Medicine Web site, www.drexelmed. edu.

3   *The Temple Daily Telegram*, December 5, 1912.

4   Bill Whitaker, *Abilene Reporter-News*, June 15, 1992.

5   Ibid.

6   Ibid.

7   John D. Pierce, "Medicine & Missions: Groundbreaking physician's full life marked by service to others," *Baptists Today*, 27, no. 10 (October 2009).

8   *The Bronco*, Simmons University yearbook, 1933, 94.

9   Ibid, 94.

10 Ibid, 253.

11 *The Bronco*, Simmons University yearbook, 1932, 221.

CHAPTER TWO

1   Dr. Russell C. Klein, *A History of LSU School of Medicine—New Orleans* (New Orleans: LSU Medical Alumni Association, 2010) Chapter 2, 1.

2   Klein, Chapter 2, 5.

3   Loyola University, Office of Public Affairs.

4   Klein, Chapter 1, 1.

5   Ibid.

6   Klein, Chapter 1, 2.

7   Klein, Chapter 2, 5.

8   Ibid.

9   Ibid.

10   Klein, 2.

11   Ibid.

12   Klein, 3.

13   Klein, 9.

14   Baylor College of Medicine, Michael E. DeBakey Department of Surgery, http://www.debakeydepartmentofsurgery.org (accessed April 23, 2011).

15   Ibid.

16   Eleanor Sellers Hoppe, "Highlights From the History of the Taylor-Jones-Haskell County Medical Society: A Century of Leadership in Health Care," *Taylor-Jones-Haskell County Medical Society: A Century of Healing*: 295.

17   *Abilene Reporter-News*, June 13, 1988.

18   Ibid.

19   Ibid.

CHAPTER THREE

1   *Abilene Reporter-News*, October 30, 1988.

2   Ibid.

3   National Library of Medicine, National Institutes of Health, http://www.nlm.nih.gov (accessed April 23, 2011).

4   Elizabeth Silverthorne, *Women Pioneers in Texas Medicine* (Texas A&M University Press, 1997) introduction.

5   Ibid.

6   Ibid.

7   Ibid.

8   Ibid.

9   Sylvia Van Voast Ferris and Eleanor Sellers Hoppe. *Scalpels and Sabers: Nineteenth Century Medicine in Texas* (Austin: Eakin Press, 1985), 198.

10 University of Texas Medical Branch School of Nursing, "120th Anniversary," http://www.son.utmb.edu/about/120anniversary.cfm (accessed April 23, 2011).

11 *Abilene Reporter-News*, August 1, 1940.

12 Ibid.

13 *Abilene Reporter-News*, August 14, 1940.

14 *Abilene Reporter-News*, August 3, 1940.

15 Ibid.

16 *Abilene Reporter-News*, August 3, 1940.

17 Ibid., 5.

18 *Abilene Reporter-News*, August 2, 1940.

19 Ibid., 9

20 *Abilene Reporter-News*, August 1, 1940.

21 *Texas State Journal of Medicine*, XXXV (May 1939–April 1940): 904.

22 *Abilene Reporter-News*, November 26, 1940.

23 James M. Myers, *The Handbook of Texas Online* (Austin: Texas State Historical Association), http://www.tshaonline.org (accessed April 23, 2011).

24 Ibid.

25 Ibid.

26 *Worley's Abilene City Directory 1941* (Dallas: John F. Worley Directory Co., Publishers, 1941), 88.

27 *Worley's Abilene City Directory 1941* (Dallas: John F. Worley Directory Co., Publishers, 1941), 87.

28 John Lacy Beckham, *The Handbook of Texas Online* (Austin: Texas State Historical Association), http://www.tshaonline.org (accessed April 23, 2011).

29 Ibid.

CHAPTER FOUR

1 *Worley's Abilene City Directory 1946* (Dallas: John F. Worley Directory Co., Publishers, 1946), 87.

2 Advertisement, *Texas State Journal of Medicine* XXXVIII 3 (July 1942): 40.

3 Ibid, 41.

4 Advertisement, *Texas State Journal of Medicine,* XXXVI 7 (November 1940): 19.

5 *Texas State Journal of Medicine,* XLII (May 1946–April 1947): 664.

CHAPTER FIVE

1 *Abilene Reporter-News*, November 10, 1948.

2 *Abilene Reporter-News*, March 20, 1949.

3 *Abilene Reporter-News*, September 6, 1981.

4 "Hendrick History." http://www.ehendrick.org/history (accessed April 23, 2011)

5 "Earl M. Collier Award," http://www.tha.org/HealthCareProviders/AboutTHA/History (accessed April 23, 2011).

6 "Boone Powell, Jr., MPH, FACHE: a conversation with the editor," Volume 14, Number 1, January 2001, http://www.baylorhealth.edu/proceedings/14_1/14_1powellinterview.html (accessed April 23, 2011).

7   "Bryce Jordan (1983-1990)," http://www.libraries.psu.edu (accessed April 23, 2011).

CHAPTER SIX

1   Melba McNeil, M.D. "Congenital Diaphragmatic Hernia on the Right Involving the Ascending Part of the Colon," *The Archives of Pediatrics & Adolescent Medicine*, formerly the *American Journal of Diseases of Children* 73 (1947), http://archpedi.ama-assn.org (accessed April 23, 2011).

2   *Abilene Reporter-News*, October 30, 1988.

3   "Hendrick Home for Children," http://www.hendrickhome.com (accessed April 23, 2011).

CHAPTER SEVEN

1   Katharyn Duff, *Abilene Reporter-News*, January 13, 1959.

2   Ibid.

3   Ibid.

4   Ibid.

5   *Abilene Reporter-News*, October 16, 1956.

6   Ibid.

7   Duff, *Abilene Reporter-News*, January 13, 1959.

8   *Abilene Reporter-News*, December 29, 1961.

9   Ibid.

10 Ibid.

11 Ibid.

12 *Abilene Reporter-News*, February 22, 1958.

13 *Abilene Reporter-News*, August 22, 1975.

14 *Abilene Reporter-News*, January 2, 1960.

15 Ibid.

16 Enid Nemy, "Liz Carpenter, Journalist, Feminist and Johnson Aide, Dies at 89," *New York Times* Web site, March 21, 2010, http://www.nytimes.com/2010/03/21/us/politics/21carpenter.html (accessed April 23, 2011)

17 Ibid.

18 Ibid.

19 Ibid.

20 Ibid.

21 Ibid.

22 Loretta Fulton, *Abilene Reporter-News*, September 20, 2003.

23 Ibid.

CHAPTER EIGHT

1 Geraldine Satterwhite, *Abilene Reporter-News*, July 24, 1983.

2 Brien Murphy, *Abilene Reporter-News*, July 12, 2007.

3 Ibid.

4 Live Auctioneers, http://www.liveauctioneers.com/item/68456 (accessed April 23, 2011).

CHAPTER NINE

1 Joakim Garff, author; Bruce H. Kirmmse, translator. *Soren Kierkegaard: A Biography* (Princeton, NJ: Princeton University Press, English translation 2005).

2 *Abilene Reporter-News*, May 24, 1962.

3 Ibid.

4 Vijaya Lakshmi Pandit Biography, copyright 1994-2010 *Encyclopaedia Britannica,* www.biography.com.

5   Ibid.

6   Ibid.

7   Landrum Bolling, "D. Elton Trueblood: December 12, 1900 to December 20, 1994, http://www.waynet.org/people/biography/trueblood.htm (accessed April 23, 2011).

8   Ibid.

CHAPTER TEN

1   Drexel University College of Medicine Web site, http://www.drexelmed.edu (accessed April 23, 2011).

2   Merle Watson, *Abilene Reporter-News*, January 10, 1983.

3   Pat Kilpatrick, *Abilene Reporter-News*, July 8, 1979.

4   Ibid.

5   Ibid.

6   L.A. Chung, *San Jose Mercury News* Web site, Wednesday, March 29, 2006, http://www.mercurynews.com (accessed April 23, 2011).

7   Ibid.

8   National Women's History Project Web site, http://www.nwhp.org (accessed April 23, 2011).

9   "President Remembers University's Influences," February 15, 2002, Oklahoma Baptist University http://www.okbu.edu (accessed April 23, 2011).

CHAPTER ELEVEN

1   John D. Pierce, "Medicine & Missions: Groundbreaking physician's full life marked by service to others," *Baptists Today*, 27, no. 10 (October 2009) .

CHAPTER TWELVE

1 Robison (Rob) B. James, Barbara Jackson, Robert E. Shepherd, Jr., and Cornelia Showalter, *The Fundamentalist Takeover in the Southern Baptist Convention: A Brief History* (Macon, Georgia: Cooperative Baptist Fellowship of Georgia, 2006) http://www.sbctakeover.com (accessed April 23, 2011).

2 Ibid.

3 Ibid.

4 Ibid.

5 Ibid.

6 Roy A. Jones II, *Abilene Reporter-News*, March 14, 1992.

7 Ibid.

CHAPTER THIRTEEN

1 A. Yvonne Stackhouse, Hardin-*Simmons University: A Centennial History* (Abilene, Texas: Hardin-Simmons University, 1991), 285-286.

2 Ibid.

3 Hall of Leaders induction citation, Hardin-Simmons University, 2004.

4 Ibid.

5 Loretta Fulton, *Abilene Reporter-News*, April 19, 2009.

CHRONOLOGY

December 4, 1912	Born, Temple, Texas
1929	Graduates Temple High School
1929-30	Attends Temple Junior College
1930	Enrolls as sophomore at Simmons University, Abilene, Texas; lives with uncle and his wife, Dr. W.R. Snow and Mae Cagle Snow
June 7, 1933	Graduates Simmons University with bachelor's degree in chemistry and education
September 3, 1933	Marries Fred Boyd, who worked for Virginia's uncle, Dr. W.R. Snow, while attending McMurry College; both enroll at Louisiana State University School of Medicine
May 31, 1937	Earns Bachelor of Medicine degree and begins internship
1937-1938	Serves internship at Charity Hospital, New Orleans
May 30, 1938	Earns Doctor of Medicine degree
1938-39	Serves residency at Charity Hospital
November 1939	Receives license to practice medicine in Texas
September 1940	Opens office in Mims Building, 1049 North Third Street, Abilene
May 9, 1944	Daughter, Ann Virginia (Genna) Boyd, born in Temple
1948	Divorced from Fred Boyd
Nov. 9, 1948	Elected president of the Taylor-Jones County Medical Society
July 7, 1953	Marries Abilene oilman Ed Connally
Dec. 16, 1958	Elected chairman of the staff of St. Ann Hospital
Dec. 16, 1960	Elected chief of staff of Hendrick Memorial Hospital to serve in 1961

May 22, 1962	Virginia's mother, Stella V. Hawkins, dies
1973	Receives Distinguished Alumna Award from Hardin-Simmons University
August 21, 1975	Ed Connally dies at age 66
September 24, 1975	Virginia's father, N. Lee Hawkins, dies
1977	Named to Hardin-Simmons University Board of Trustees, serving until 1987
1981	Begins service on National Board of the Medical College of Pennsylvania, established in 1850 as the Female Medical College of Pennsylvania, the first in the world for women physicians.
1981	Establishes the Connally Endowed Professorship of Missions at Hardin-Simmons University
1981	Receives Keeter Alumni Service Award from Hardin-Simmons University
November 1981	Receives "1981 Special Friend Award" from the University of Texas School of Nursing Advisory Council for her contributions to the nursing profession and to the UT-Austin Nursing School.
1982	Closes medical practice after 42 years
1984	Named Medical Director and Senior Vice President of Hardin-Simmons University's Fairleigh Dickenson Science Research Center, serving until it closed in 1989
1988	Named to Board of Development at Hardin-Simmons University
October 1988	Recipient of one of the original Pathfinder Awards given by the YWCA and the *Abilene Reporter-News.*
1988	Connally Endowed Professorship of Missions at Hardin-Simmons University upgraded to Chair, with Dr. Jesse C. Fletcher as first holder of the chair

166

1989	Receives honorary Doctor of Humanities Degree from Hardin-Simmons University
2000	Connally Missions Center dedicated at Hardin-Simmons University
2004	Named to Hall of Leaders at Hardin-Simmons University
2004	Receives Pioneer in Medicine award at the 100th anniversary celebration of the Taylor-Jones-Haskell County Medical Society
December 4, 2007	Mayor Norm Archibald proclaims "Dr. Virginia Connally Day' in honor of her 95th birthday; Gov. Rick Perry proclaims Virginia a "Yellow Rose of Texas," to which Virginia quipped, "That's going to look good in my obituary."
April 23, 2009	Named inaugural recipient of Abilene Woman's Club Legacy Award
September 2010	At age 97, Virginia embarks on eighth trip to Finland with Genna, granddaughter Sundi Spivey, and grandson Sid Roberts
December 4, 2010	Surrounded by family and friends, Virginia celebrates 98th birthday over three days, thanks to Genna's skillful planning
February 22, 2011	Named inaugural recipient of the Virtue Award given by the Roundtable organization at Hardin-Simmons University at its centennial luncheon

BY LORETTA FULTON

INDEX